A Christian on the Mount

A Treatise Concerning Meditation

by Thomas Watson

(1620-1686)

"His delight is in the law of the Lord, and on his law he meditates day and night." Psalm 1:2

Having led you through the Chamber of Delight in my previous discourse, I will now bring you into the Withdrawing Room of Meditation. "In his law does he meditate day and night."

I. The opening of the Words, and the Proposition asserted.

Grace breeds delight in God, and delight breeds meditation. Meditation is a duty wherein consists the essentials of religion, and which nourishes the very life-blood of it. That the Psalmist may show how much the godly man is habituated to this blessed work of meditation, he subjoins, "In his law does he meditate day and night;" not but that there may be sometimes intermission: God allows time for our calling, he grants some relaxation; but when it is said, the godly man meditates day and night, the meaning is, frequently—he is much conversant in the duty.

It is a command of God to pray without ceasing, 1 Thess. 5:17. The meaning is—not that we should be always praying—but that we should every day set some time apart for prayer. We read in the Old law it was called the continual sacrifice, Numb. 28:24, not that the people of Israel did nothing else but sacrifice—but because they had their stated hours, every morning and evening they offered, therefore it was called the continual sacrifice. Thus the godly man is said to meditate day and night, that is, he is often at this work, he is no stranger to meditation.

Doctrine. The proposition that results out of the text is this—that a godly Christian is a meditating Christian, Psalm 119:15. "I will meditate in your precepts." 1 Tim. 4:15, "Meditate upon these things." Meditation is the chewing upon the truths we have heard. The beasts in the old law which did not chew the cud, were unclean; the professor who does not by meditation chew the cud, is to be accounted unclean. Meditation is like the watering of the seed, it makes the fruits of grace to flourish.

II. Showing the NATURE of Meditation.

If it be inquired what meditation is, I answer—Meditation is the soul's retiring of itself, that by a serious and solemn thinking upon God, the heart may be raised up to heavenly affections. This description has three branches.

1. Meditation is the soul's retiring of itself. A Christian, when he goes to meditate, must lock up himself from the world. The world spoils meditation; Christ went by himself into the mountainside to pray, Matt. 14:23, so, go into a solitary place when you are to meditate. "Isaac went out to meditate in the field," Gen. 24:63; he sequestered and retired himself that he might take a walk with God by meditation. Zaccheus had a mind to see Christ, and he got out of the crowd, "He ran before, and climbed up into a sycamore tree to see him," Luke 19:3, 4. So, when we would see God, we must get out of the crowd of worldly business; we must climb up into the tree by retiredness of meditation, and there we shall have the best prospect of heaven.

The world's music will either play us asleep, or distract us in our meditations. When a mote has gotten into the eye—it hinders the sight. Just so, when worldly thoughts, as motes, are gotten into the mind, which is the eye of the soul—it cannot look up so steadfastly to heaven by contemplation. Therefore, as when Abraham went to sacrifice, "he left his servant and the donkey at the bottom of the hill," Gen. 22:5, so, when a Christian is going up the hill of meditation, he should leave all secular cares at the bottom of the hill, that he may be alone, and take a turn in heaven. If the wings of the bird are full of slime, she cannot fly. Meditation is the wing of the soul; when a Christian is beslimed with earth, he cannot fly to God upon this wing. Bernard when he came to the church-door, used to say, "Stay here all my worldly thoughts, that I may converse with God in the temple." So say to yourself, "I am going now to meditate, O all you vain thoughts stay behind, come not near!" When you are going up the mount of meditation, take heed that the world does not follow you, and throw you down from the top of this pinnacle. This is the first thing, the soul's retiring of itself—lock and bolt the door against the world.

2. The second thing in meditation, is, a serious and solemn thinking upon God. The Hebrew word to meditate, signifies with intenseness to recollect and gather together the thoughts. Meditation is not a cursory work, to have a few transient thoughts of religion; like the dogs of Nilus that lap and then run away; but there must be in meditation a fixing the heart upon the object, a steeping the thoughts. Carnal professors have their thoughts roving up and down, and will not fix on God; like the bird that hops from one branch to another, and stays in no one place. David was a man fit to meditate, "O God, my heart is fixed," Psalm 108:1.

In meditation there must be a staying of the thoughts upon the object; a man who rides quickly through a town or village—he minds nothing. But an artist who is looking on a curious piece, views the whole portraiture of it, he observes the symmetry and proportion, he minds every shadow and color. A carnal, flitting professor, is like the traveler, his thoughts ride hastily—he minds nothing of God. A wise Christian is like the artist, he views with seriousness, and ponders the things of religion, Luke 2:19. "But Mary kept all these things, and pondered them in her heart."

3. The third thing in meditation, is, the raising of the heart to holy affections. A Christian enters into meditation, as a man enters into the hospital—that he may be healed. Meditation heals the soul of its deadness and earthliness; but more of this afterwards.

III. Proving Meditation to be a DUTY.

Meditation is a duty lying upon every Christian, and there is no disputing our duty. Meditation is a duty, 1. Imposed. 2. Opposed.

1. Meditation is a duty imposed—it is not arbitrary. The same God who has bid us believe, has bid us meditate, Josh. 1:8. "This book of the law shall not depart out of your mouth—but you shall meditate therein day and night." These words, though spoken to the person of Joshua, yet they concern everyone; as the promise made to Joshua concerned all believers, Josh. 1:5 compared with Heb. 13:5. So this precept made to the person of Joshua, you shall meditate in this book of the law, takes in all Christians. As

God's Word does direct, so his will must enforce obedience.

2. Meditation is a duty opposed. We may conclude it is a good duty, because it is against the stream of corrupt nature. As one said, "you may know that religion is right—which Nero persecutes;" so you may know that is a good duty—which the heart opposes. We shall find naturally a strange averseness from meditation. We are swift to hear—but slow to meditate. To think of the world, if it were all day long, is delightful. But as for holy meditation, how does the heart wrangle and quarrel with this duty; it is like doing of penance. Now truly, there needs no other reason to prove a duty to be good, than the reluctancy of a carnal heart. To instance in the duty of "Let a man deny himself," Mat. 16:24, self-denial is as necessary as heaven—but what disputes are raised in the heart against it? What! to deny my reason, and become a fool that I may be wise; nay, not only to deny my reason—but my righteousness? What, to cast it overboard, and swim to heaven upon the plank of Christ's merits? This is such a duty that the heart does naturally oppose, and enter its dissent against. This is an argument to prove the duty of self-denial good; just so it is with this duty of meditation; the secret antipathy the heart has against it, shows it to be good; and this is reason enough to enforce meditation.

IV. Showing how Meditation differs from MEMORY.

The memory (a glorious faculty) which Aristotle calls the soul's scribe, sits and pens all things that are done. Whatever we read or hear, the memory does register; therefore, God does all his works of wonder that they may be had in remembrance. There seems to be some analogy and resemblance between meditation and memory. But I conceive there is a double difference.

1. Meditation has more sweetness in it, than the bare remembrance. The memory is the chest or cupboard to lock up a truth, meditation is the palate to feed on it. The memory is like the ark in which the manna was laid up, meditation is like Israel's eating of manna. When David began to meditate on God, it was "sweet to him as marrow," Psalm 63:5, 6. There is as much difference between a truth remembered, and a truth meditated on, as between a cordial in a glass—and a cordial drunk down.

2. The remembrance of a truth, without the serious meditation on it, will but create matter of sorrow another day. What comfort can it be to a man when he comes to die, to think he remembered many excellent notions about Christ—but never had the grace so to meditate on them, as to be transformed into them! a sermon remembered—but not ruminated, will only serve to increase our condemnation.

V. Showing how Meditation differs from STUDY.

The student's life looks like meditation—but does vary from it. Meditation and study differ three ways.

1. They differ in their nature. Study is a work of the brain, meditation of the heart; study sets the mind on work, meditation sets the heart on work.

2. They differ in their design. The design of study is notion, the design of meditation is piety. The design of study is the finding out of a truth; the design of meditation

is the spiritual improvement of a truth. The one searches for the vein of gold; the other digs out the gold.

3. They differ in the outcome and result. Study leaves a man never a whit the better; it is like a winter sun that has little warmth and influence. Meditation leaves one in a holy frame: it melts the heart when it is frozen, and makes it drop into tears of love.

VI. Showing the SUBJECTS of Meditation.

The next particular to be discussed, is the subject-matter of meditation; what a Christian should meditate upon. I am now gotten into a large field—but I shall only glance at things; I shall but do as the disciples, pluck some ears of corn as I pass along.

Some may say, "alas, I am so barren I know not what to meditate upon!" To help Christians therefore in this blessed work, I shall show you some choice select matter for meditation. There are fifteen things in the Word of God, which we should principally meditate upon.

Section 1. Meditate on God's ATTRIBUTES.

The Attributes of God are the several beams by which the divine nature shines forth to us; and there are six special attributes which we should fix our meditations upon.

Meditate upon God's OMNISCIENCE. His eye is continually upon us; he has a window open into the conscience; our thoughts are unveiled before him. He can tell the words we speak "in our bedchamber," 2 Kings 2:12.

He is described with seven eyes, to show his omniscience. "You number my steps," Job 14:16. The Hebrew word signifies to take an exact account. God is said to number our steps, when he makes a precise and critical observation of our actions; God sets down every step of our lives, and keeps as it were, a day book of all we do, and enters it down into the book. Meditate much on this omniscience.

Meditation on God's omniscience would have these effects.

1. It would be as a bridle to check and restrain us from sin. Will the thief steal—when the judge looks on?

2. Meditation on God's omniscience would be a good means to make the heart sincere. God has set a window in every man's breast, "does not he see all my ways?" Job 31:4. If I harbor proud, malicious thoughts, if I look at my own interest more than Christ's, if I juggle in my repentance—the God of heaven takes notice! Meditation on his omniscience, would make a Christian sincere, both in his actions and aims. Only a fool would dare to be a hypocrite before God!

Meditate on the HOLINESS of God. Holiness is the embroidered robe God wears: it is the glory of the Godhead, Exod. 15:11. "Glorious in holiness!" Holiness is the most orient pearl of the crown of heaven. God is the exemplar and pattern of holiness. It is primarily and originally in God as light in the sun; you may as well separate weight from lead, or heat from fire, as holiness from the divine nature; God's holiness is that whereby his heart rises against any sin, as being most diametrically opposite to his essence, Hab. 1:13. "You are of purer eyes than to behold iniquity." Meditate much on this attribute.

Meditation on God's holiness would have this effect; it would be a means to transform us into the similitude and likeness of God; God never loves us until we are like him. There is a story of a deformed man, who set lovely pictures before his wife, that seeing them she might have lovely children, and so she had. Be that as it may, while by meditation we are looking upon the beams of holiness, which are gloriously transparent in God, we shall grow like him, and be holy as he is holy. Holiness is a beautiful thing, Psalm 110. It puts a kind of angelical brightness upon us; it is the only coin which will pass current in heaven; by the frequent meditation on this attribute, we are changed into God's image.

Meditate on the WISDOM of God. He is called "the only wise God," 1 Tim. 1:17. His wisdom shines forth in the works of providence; he sits at the helm guiding all things regularly and harmoniously; he brings light out of darkness; he can strike a straight stroke by a crooked stick; he can make use of the injustice of men to do that which is just; he is infinitely wise, he breaks us by afflictions, and upon these broken pieces of the ship, brings us safely to shore; meditate on the wisdom of God.

Meditation on God's wisdom would sweetly calm our hearts.

1. When we see things go badly in the public. The all-wise God holds the reins of government in his hand; and whoever the earthly ruler—God over-rules; he knows how to turn all to good; his work will be beautiful in its season.

2. When things go badly with us in particular, the meditation on God's wisdom would rock our hearts quiet. The wise God has set me in this condition, and whether

health or sickness, his wisdom will order it for the best. God will make a golden cordial from poison, all things shall be beneficial and medicinal to me; either the Lord will expel some sin, or exercise some grace. Meditation on this would silence murmuring.

4. Meditate on the POWER of God. His power is visible in the creation. "He hangs the earth upon nothing," Job 26:7. What cannot that God do—who can create? Nothing can stand before a creating power! He needs no pre-existent matter to work upon; he needs no instruments to work with, he can work without tools; he it is before whom the angels veil their faces, and the kings of the earth cast their crowns. He it is who "removes the earth out of her place," Job 9:6. An earthquake makes the earth tremble upon her pillars—but God can shake it out of its place. God can with a word, unpin the wheels, and break the axle of the creation. He can suspend natural agents, stop the lion's mouth, cause the sun to stand still, make the fire not burn! Xerxes, the Persian monarch, threw fetters into the sea, as if he would have chained up the unruly waters; but when God commands, "the winds and sea obey him," Matt. 8:27. If he speaks the word, an army of stars appear, Judg. 5:20. If he stamps with his foot, a multitude of angels are presently in battalia; if he lifts up an ensign, and does but hiss, his very enemies shall be up in arms to revenge his quarrel, Isaiah 5:56. Who would provoke this God! "It is a fearful thing to fall into the hands of the living God," Heb. 10:31. As a lion—"he tears in pieces his adversaries," Psalm 50:22. Oh meditate on this power of God.

Meditation on God's power would be a great stay to faith. A Christian's faith may anchor safely upon the rock of God's power. It was Samson's riddle, "Out of the strong came forth sweetness;" Judges 14:14. While we are 'itating on the power of God, out of this strong comes h sweetness. Is the church of God low? he can "create .ises in Jerusalem," Isaiah 65:28. Is your corruption ong? God can break the head of this leviathan. Is your eart as hard as a stone? God can dissolve it. "The Almighty makes my heart soft." Faith triumphs in the power of God: out of this strong comes forth sweetness. Abraham meditating on God's power, did not stagger through unbelief, Romans 4:20. He knew God could make a dead womb fruitful, and dry breasts give suck.

5. Meditate upon the MERCY of God. Mercy is an innate disposition in God to do good; as the sun has an innate property to shine, Psalm 86:5. "You Lord are good, and ready to forgive, and plenteous in mercy to all them that call upon you. God's mercy is so sweet, that it makes all his other attributes sweet. Holiness without mercy, and justice without mercy, would be dreadful. Geographers write that the city of Syracuse in Sicily is curiously situated, that the sun is never out of sight; though the children of God are under some clouds of affliction, yet the sun of mercy is never quite out of sight. God's justice reaches to the clouds; his mercy reaches above the clouds.

How slow is God to anger. He was longer in destroying Jericho, than in making the world; he made the world in six days—but he was seven days in demolishing the walls of Jericho. How many warning arrows did God shoot against Jerusalem, before he shot off his destroying arrow? Justice goes by foot, Gen. 18:21. Mercy has wings. The sword of justice often lies a long time in the scabbard, and rusts, until sin draws it out and sharpens it against a nation. God's justice is like the widow's oil, which ran a while, and ceased, 1 Kings 4:6. God's mercy is like Aaron's oil, which rested not on his head—but ran down to the skirts of his garment, Psalm 133:2. So the golden oil of God's mercy does not rest upon the head of a godly parent—but is often poured on his children, and so runs down, "To the third and fourth generation," even the borders of a pious seed. Often meditate upon the mercy of God.

Meditation on mercy would be a powerful loadstone to draw sinners to God by repentance. It would be as a cork to the net—to keep the heart from sinking in despair. Behold a city of refuge to fly to—"God is the Father of mercies," 2 Cor. 1:3. Mercy does as naturally issue from him, as the child from the parent. God "delights in mercy," Micah 7:18. Chrysostom says, it is delightful to the mother to have her breasts drawn; and how delightful is it to God to have the breasts of mercy drawn! Mercy finds out the worst sinner; mercy comes not only with salvation in its hand—but with healing under its wings.

Meditation on God's mercy would melt a sinner into tears: One reading a pardon sent to him from the king, fell a weeping, and burst out into these words, "A pardon has done that which death could not do, it has made my heart relent."

6. Meditate upon the TRUTH of God. Mercy makes the promise, and Truth performs it, Psalm 89:33, "I will not allow my faithfulness to fail." God can as well deny himself as his word. He is "abundant in truth," Exod. 34:6. That is—if God has made a promise of mercy to his people, he will be so far from coming short of his Word, that he will be better than his Word. God often does more than he has said, never less; he often shoots beyond the mark of the promise he has set, never short of it. He is abundant in truth. God may sometimes delay a promise, he will not

deny it. The promise may lie a long time as seed hidden under ground—but it is all the while a ripening. The promise of Israel's deliverance lay four hundred and thirty years under ground; but when the time was come, the promise did not go a day beyond its reckoning, Exod. 12:41. "The strength of Israel will not lie," 1 Sam. 15:29. Meditation on God's truth would—

1. Be a pillar of support for faith. The world hangs upon God's power, and faith hangs upon his truth.

2. Meditation on God's truth would make us ambitious to imitate him. We should be true in our words, true in our dealings. Pythagoras being asked, "What makes men like God?" answered, "When they speak truth."

Section 2. Meditate upon the PROMISES of God.

The promises of God are flowers growing in the paradise of scripture; meditation, like the bee, sucks out the sweetness of them. The promises are of no use or comfort to us, until they are meditated upon. Roses hanging in the garden may give a fragrant redolence, yet their sweet water is distilled only by the fire. Just so, the promises are sweet in reading over—but the water of these roses, the spirits and quintessence of the promises, are distilled into the soul only by meditation. The incense, when it is pounded and beaten, smells sweetest. Meditating on a promise, like the beating of the incense, makes it more fragrant and pleasant. The promises may be compared to a gold mine, which only enriches when the gold is dug out. By holy meditation, we dig out that spiritual gold which lies hidden in the midst of the promise, and so we come to be enriched!

Cardan says that every precious gem-stone has some hidden virtue in it. They are called precious promises, 2 Pet. 1:4. When they are applied by meditation, then their virtue appears, and they become precious indeed. There are three sorts of promises which we should meditate upon.

1. Promises of REMISSION. "I, even I am he who blots out your transgressions for my own sake, and will not remember your sins," Isaiah 43:25. Whereas the poor sinner may say, "Alas, I am deep in debt with God, I fear I have not filled his bottle with my tears—but I have filled his book with my debts!" Well, but meditate on his promise, "I am he who blots out," etc. The word there in the original to blot out, is a metaphor alluding to a merchant, who when his debtor has paid him, he blots out the debt, and gives him an acquittance. So says God, "I will blot out your sin, I will cross out the debt-book!" In the Hebrew it is, "I am blotting out your transgressions." "I have taken my pen, and am crossing out your debt!" Oh, but may the sinner say, "There is no reason God should do thus for me." Well, but acts of grace do not go by reason, "I will blot out your sins—for my name's sake." Oh, but says the sinner, "Will not the Lord call my sins again to remembrance?" No, he promises to send them into oblivion; "I will not upbraid you with your sins—I will remember your sins no more." Here is a sweet promise to meditate upon; it is a hive full of the honey of the gospel.

2. Meditate upon promises of SANCTIFICATION. The earth is not so apt to be overgrown with weeds and thorns, as the heart is to be overgrown with lusts! Now, God has made many promises of healing, Hos. 14:4, and purging, Jer. 33:8. Promises of sending his Spirit, Isaiah 44:3, which, for its sanctifying nature, is compared sometimes to water which cleanses the vessel; sometimes

to wind, which is the fan to winnow and purify the air; sometimes to fire, which refines the metals. Meditate often on that promise, Isaiah 1:18, "Though your sins be as scarlet—they shall be as white as snow!" Scarlet is so deep a dye, that all the art of man cannot take it out; but behold here a promise—God will whiten the soul; he will make a scarlet sinner—into a snow white saint! By virtue of this refining and consecrating work, a Christian is made partaker of the divine nature; he has a suitability and fitness to have communion with God forever. Meditate much on this promise.

3. Meditate upon promises of REMUNERATION. "The haven of rest," Heb. 4:9. The beatifical sight of God, Matt. 5:8. The glorious mansions, John 14:2. Meditation on these promises will be as choice cordials to keep us from fainting under our sins and sorrows.

Section 3. Meditate upon the Love of Christ.

Christ is full of love, as he is of merit. What was it but love—that he should save us—and not the fallen angels? Among the rarities of the loadstone, this is not the least—that leaving the gold and pearl, it should draw iron to it—which is a baser kind of metal. Just so, that Christ should leave the angels, those more noble spirits, the gold and pearl—and draw mankind to him—how does this proclaim his love? Love was the wing on which he flew into the virgin's womb!

1. How TRANSCENDENT is Christ's love to the saints! The apostle calls it a love "which passes knowledge," Eph. 3:19. It is such a love as God the Father bears to Christ; the same for quality, though not equality, John 15:9. "As the Father has loved me—so have I loved

you." A believer's heart is the garden where Christ has planted this sweet flower of his love. It is the channel through which the golden stream of his affection runs.

2. How SOVEREIGN is Christ's love! "Brothers, think of what you were when you were called. Not many of you were wise by human standards; not many were influential; not many were of noble birth." 1 Corinthians 1:26 In the old law God passed by the noble lion and the eagle—and took the dove for sacrifice. That God should pass by so many of noble birth and abilities, and that the lot of free grace should fall upon me—O the depth of divine grace!

3. How INVINCIBLE is the love of Christ! "It is strong as death," Cant. 8:6. Death might take away Christ's life—but not his love! Neither can our sin wholly quench that divine flame of love; the church had her infirmities, her sleepy fits, Cant. 5:2, but though blacked and sullied, yet she is still a dove; Christ could see the faith, and wink at the failing. He who painted Alexander, drew him with his finger over the scar on his face. Just so, Christ puts the finger of mercy upon the scars of the saints! He will not throw away his pearls for every speck of dirt! That which makes this love of Christ the more stupendous, is that there was nothing in us to excite or draw forth his love! He did not love us because we were worthy—but by loving us he made us worthy!

4. How IMMUTABLE is Christ's love! "Having loved his own, he loved them to the end," John 13:1. The saints are like letters of gold engraved upon Christ's heart, which cannot be erased out. Meditate much upon the love of Christ.

1. Serious meditation on the love of Christ, would make us love him in return. "Can one go upon hot coals, and his feet not be burnt?" Proverbs 6:28. Who can tread by meditation upon these hot coals of Christ's love, and his heart not burn in love to him?

2. Meditation on Christ's love, would set our eyes abroach with tears for our gospel unkindnesses. O that we should sin against so sweet a Savior! had we none to abuse—but our best friend? Had we nothing to kick against—but affections of love? Did not Christ suffer enough upon the cross—but must we needs make him suffer more? Do we give him more gall and vinegar to drink? O, if anything can dissolve the heart into mourning, it is the unkindness offered to Christ. When Peter thought of Christ's love to him—Christ could deny Peter nothing, yet he could deny Christ, this made his eyes to water; "Peter went out and wept bitterly."

3. Meditation on Christ's love would make us love our enemies. Jesus Christ showed love to his enemies. We read of "the fire licking up the water," 1 Kings 18:38. It is usual for water to quench the fire, but for fire to dry up and consume the water, which was not capable of burning, this was miraculous! Such a miracle did Christ show; his love burned where there was no fit matter to work upon—nothing but sin and enmity. He loved his enemies; the fire of his love consumed and licked up the water of their sins! He prayed for his enemies, "Father forgive them;" he shed his tears—for those who shed his blood! Those who gave him gall and vinegar to drink—to them he gave his sin-forgiving blood to drink. Meditation on his love—should melt our hearts in love to our enemies. Augustine says, "Christ made a pulpit of the cross, and the great lesson he taught Christians was, to love their enemies."

4. Meditation on Christ's love would be a means to support us in case of his absence. Sometimes he is pleased to withdraw himself, Cant. 5:6, yet when we consider how entire and immutable his love is, it will make us wait with patience until he sweetly manifests himself to us. He is love, and he cannot forsake his people very long, Micah 7:19. The sun may be gone a while from our climate—but it returns in the spring. Meditation on Christ's love may make us wait for the return of this Sun of Righteousness; Heb. 10:37, "For yet a little while and he who shall come will come." He is truth, therefore he shall come; he is love, therefore he will come.

Section 4. Meditate upon SIN.

1. Meditate on the GUILT of sin. We are in Adam as in a common head, or root—and he sinning, we become guilty, Romans 5:12, "Therefore, just as sin entered the world through one man, and death through sin, and in this way death came to all men, because all sinned." By his treason—our blood is tainted. This guilt brings shame with it, as its twin! Romans 6:21.

2. Meditate upon the FILTH of sin. Not only is the guilt of Adam's sin imputed, but the poison of his nature is disseminated to us! Our virgin nature is defiled! If the heart is spotted—how then can the actions be pure? If the water in the well is foul—it cannot be clean in the bucket! Isaiah 64:6, "We are all as an unclean thing." We are like a patient under the physician's care—who has no sound part in him, his head is bruised, his liver is swelled, his lungs are gasping, his blood is infected, his feet are gangrened. Thus is it with us before saving grace comes! In the mind there is darkness! In the memory there is slipperiness! In the heart there is hardness! In the will there is stubborness! "You are

sick from head to foot—covered with bruises, welts, and infected wounds—without any ointments or bandages!" Isaiah 1:6. A sinner befilthied with sin, is no better than a devil in man's shape!

And which is sadly to be laid to heart--is the adherency of this sin. Sin is natural to us. The apostle calls it, "the sin that so easily ensnares us!" Heb. 12:1. Sin is not easily cast off. A man may as well shake off the skin of his body—as the sin of his soul! There is no shaking off this viper until death!

Oh, often meditate on this contagion of sin. How strong is that poison—a drop whereof is able to poison a whole sea? How venomous and malignant was that apple—a taste of which poisoned all mankind! Meditate sadly on this. Meditation on sin would make the plumes of pride fall off! If our knowledge makes us proud—that is sin enough to make us humble. The best saint alive who is taken out of the grave of sin—yet has the smell of the grave-clothes still upon him!

3. Meditate upon the CURSE of sin. Gal. 3:10. "Cursed is everyone who does not continue to do everything written in the Book of the Law." This curse is like a deadly canker upon fruit, which keeps it from thriving. Sin is not only a defiling thing—but a damning thing! It is not only a spot in the face—but a stab at the heart! Sin betrays us into the devil's hands—who writes all his laws in blood. Sin binds us over to the wrath of God! What then, are all our earthly enjoyments—with the sword of divine vengeance hanging over our head! Sin brings forth the "scroll written with curses" against a sinner, Zech. 5:5, and it is a "flying scroll"—it comes swiftly—if mercy does not stop it. "You are cursed with a curse!" Mat. 3:9.

Thus it is until the head of this curse is cut off by Christ. Oh meditate upon this curse due to sin.

1. Meditation on this curse would make us afraid of retaining sin. When Micah had stolen his mother's money, and heard her curse him, he dared not keep it any longer, but restored it, Judg. 17:2. He was afraid of his mother's curse; what then is God's curse!

2. Meditation on this curse would make us afraid of entertaining sin. We would not willingly entertain one in our house who had a deadly plague! Sin brings along with it, the plague of God's curse, which cleaves to a sinner. Meditation on this, would make us fly from sin! While we sit under the shadow of this bramble of sin—fire will come out of the bramble eternally to devour us! Judg. 9:15.

Section 5. Meditate upon the Vanity of the CREATURE.

When you have sifted out the finest flour that the creature can give, you will find something either to dissatisfy or nauseate. The best wine has its froth, the sweetest rose has its prickles, and the purest comforts have their dregs. The creature cannot be said to be full—unless we say that it is full of vanity; as a sail may be filled with wind. Job 20:22, "At the height of his success distress will come to him; the full weight of misery will crush him." Those who think to find happiness here on earth, are like Apollo who embraced a tree, instead of the lovely Daphne. Meditate on this vanity of the creature. The world is like a broken looking glass—which shows a false beauty.

1. Meditation on worldly vanity would be like the digging about the roots of a tree, to loosen it from the earth.

It would much loosen our hearts from the world, and be an excellent preservative against the love of earthly things. Let a Christian think thus with himself, "Why am I so serious about such a worthless vanity? if the whole earth were changed into a globe of gold, it could not fill my heart!"

2. Meditation on the creature's vanity would make us look after more solid comforts—the favor of God, the blood of Christ, the influences of the Spirit. When I see that the life which I fetch from the cistern is vain—I will go the more to the ocean! In Christ there is an inexhaustible treasury! When a man finds the bough begin to break, he lets go of the bough, and catches hold on the trunk of the tree. Just so, when we find the creature to be but a rotten bough, then by faith we shall catch hold on Christ, the tree of life! Rev. 2:7. The creature is but a shaking reed, God is the immoveable rock of ages!

Section 6. Meditate on the Excellency of GRACE.

1. Grace is precious in itself. 2. Pet. 1:1, precious faith.

1. Grace is precious, in its original, it comes from above, James 3:17.

2. Grace is precious, in its nature; it is the seed of God, 1 John 3:9. Grace is the spiritual embroidery of the soul; it is the very signature and engraving of the Holy Spirit. Grace does not lose its color: it is such a commodity, that the longer we keep it, the better it is—it changes into glory!

2. As grace is precious in itself, so it makes us precious to God; as a rich diamond adorns the one who

wears it. Isaiah 43:4, 'Since you were precious in my sight." The saints who are invested with grace, are God's jewels, Mal. 3:17, though sullied with reproach, though besmeared with blood—yet, jewels! All the world besides, is but chaff. These are the jewels—and heaven is the golden cabinet where they shall be locked up safe! A gracious man is the glory of the age he lives in. So illustrious in God's eye is a soul bespangled with grace, that he does not think the world worthy of him, Heb. 11:38, "Of whom the world was not worthy." Therefore God calls his people home so fast, because they are too good to live in the world, Proverbs 2:26, "The righteous is more excellent than his neighbor."

Grace is the best blessing; it has a transcendency above all other things. There are two things which sparkle much in our eyes—but grace infinitely outshines both.

1. GOLD. The sun does not shine so much in our eyes as gold; it is the mirror of beauty, "money answers all things," Eccl. 10:19. But grace weighs heavier than gold; gold draws the heart from God, grace draws the heart to God. Gold does but enrich the mortal part, grace the angelic part. Gold perishes, 1 Pet. 1:7, grace perseveres. The rose, the fuller it is blown, the sooner it sheds—is an emblem of all things, besides grace.

2. GIFTS. These are nature's pride. Gifts and abilities, like Rachel, are fair to look upon—but grace excels. I had rather be holy than eloquent. An heart full of grace, is better than an head full of notions. Gifts commend no man to God. It is not the skin of the apple we esteem, though of a vermilion color—but the fruit. We judge not the better of a horse for his trappings and ornaments, unless he has good mettle. What are the most glorious abilities, if there is not the metal of grace in the heart? Gifts may be bestowed

upon one for the good of others, as the nurse's breasts are given her for the child—but grace is bestowed for a man's own eternal advantage. God may send away reprobates with gifts, as Abraham gave the sons of the concubines some gifts, Gen. 25:6—but he entails the inheritance only upon grace. O, often meditate upon the excellency of grace!

1. The musing on the beauty of grace would make us fall in LOVE with it. He who meditates on the worth of a diamond, grows in love with it. Damascen calls the graces of the Spirit the very characters and impressions of the divine nature. Grace is that flower of delight, which, like the vine in the parable, Judg. 9:13, "cheers the heart of God and man."

2. Meditation on the excellency of grace would make us earnest in the PURSUIT after it. We dig for gold in the mine, we sweat for it in the furnace. Did we meditate on the worth of grace, we would dig in the mine of ordinances for it. What sweating and wrestling in prayer would we have! We would put on a modest boldness, and not take a denial. "What will you give me (says Abraham) seeing I go childless?" Gen. 15:2. So would the soul say, "Lord, what will you give me, seeing I go graceless? Who will give me to drink of the water of the well of life?"

3. Meditation on the excellency of grace would make us endeavor to be instrumental to CONVEY grace to others. Is grace so transcendently precious, and have I a child who lacks grace? Oh that I might be a means to convey this treasure into his soul! I have read of a rich Florentine, who being about to die, called all his sons together, and used these words to them, "It much rejoices me now upon my death-bed, that I shall leave you all wealthy;" but a parent's ambition should be rather to

convey sanctity, that he may say, "O my children, it rejoices me that I shall leave you gracious; it comforts me that before I die, I shall see Jesus Christ live in you."

Section 7. Meditate upon your SPIRITUAL STATE.

Enter into a serious meditation on the state of your souls; while you are meditating on other things, do not forget yourselves; the great work lies at home. It was Solomon's advice, "know the state of your flock," Proverbs 27:23, much more know the state of your soul; for lack of this meditation, men are like travelers, skilled in other countries—but ignorant of their own: so they know other things—but know not how it goes with their souls, whether they are in a good state or bad; there are few who by holy meditation, enter within themselves. There are two reasons why so few meditate upon the state of their souls.

1. Self-guiltiness. Men are reluctant to look into their hearts by meditation, lest they should find that which would trouble them. The cup is in their sack. Most are herein like tradesmen, who being ready to sink in their estates, are reluctant; to look into their account books, lest they should find their estate low; but had you not better enter into your heart by meditation, than God should in a sad manner enter into judgment with you?

2. Presumption. Men hope all is well; men will not take their land upon trust—but will have it surveyed; yet they will take their spiritual estate upon trust, without any surveying. They are confident their case is good; Proverbs 14:16. They presume that it is a thing not to be disputed on, and this confidence is but conceit. The foolish virgins, though they had no oil in their lamps, yet how confident were they? "They came knocking"—they doubted not of

admittance. Just so, many do not possess salvation—but remain secure; they presume all is well, never seriously meditating whether they have oil or not. O Christian, meditate about your soul! See how the case stands between God and you; do as merchants, cast up your estate, that you may see what you are worth. See if you are rich towards God, Luke 12:21. Meditate about three things:

1. About your debts, see if your debts are paid or not, that is, your sins pardoned; see if there be no arrears, no sin in your soul unrepented of.

2. Meditate about your will; see if your will is made yet. Have you resigned up all the interest in yourself? Have you given up your love to God? Have you given up your will? This is to make your will. Meditate about your will; make your spiritual will in the time of health; if you put off the making of your will until death, it may be invalid; perhaps God will not accept of your soul then.

3. Meditate about your evidences. These evidences are the graces of the Spirit; see whether you have any evidences. What desires have you after Christ? what faith? see whether there are any flaws in your evidences; are your desires true? do you as well desire heavenly principles, as heavenly privileges? O meditate seriously upon your evidences.

To sift our hearts thus by meditation, is very necessary; if we find our estate is not sound, the mistake is discovered, and the danger can be prevented. If our spiritual estate is sound, we shall have the comfort of it. What gladness was it to Hezekiah, when he could say, "Remember now, O Lord, how I have walked before you in truth, and with a perfect heart, and have done that which is good in your sight," Isaiah 38:3. So, what unspeakable comfort will it be, when a Christian, upon a serious meditation and review of his spiritual condition, can say, "I have something to show for heaven—I know I have passed from death to life," 1 John 3:14, and as a holy man once said, "I am Christ's, and the devil has nothing to do with me."

Section 8. Meditate upon the small number of those who shall be saved.

The eighth subject of meditation is, the small number that shall be saved; "but few are chosen," Mat. 20:16. Among the millions in Rome—there are but few senators; and among the swarms of people in the world—there are but few believers. One said, all the names of the good emperors might be engraved in a little ring. There are not many names in the book of life. We read of four kinds of ground in the parable, and but one good ground, Matt. 13. How few in the world know Christ. How few that believe in him? Who has believed our report? Isaiah 53:1. How few bow to Christ's scepter. The heathen idolaters and Mahometans possess almost all Asia, Africa, America; in many parts of the world the devil is worshiped, as among the Parthians and Pilapians; Satan takes up most climates—and hearts. How many formalists are in the world? 2 Tim. 3:5, "having a form of godliness." Formalists are like wool which receives a slight tincture, not a deep dye, whose religion is a paint—not an engraving, (which a storm of persecution will wash off). These look like Christ's doves—but are the serpent's brood. They hate God's image, like the panther, that hates the picture of a man.

O often meditate on the small number of those who shall be saved.

1. Meditation on this, would keep us from marching along with the multitude. "You shall not follow a multitude," Exod. 23:2. The multitude usually goes wrong: most men walk "after the course of this world," Eph. 2:2. That is, the lusts of their hearts, and the fashions of the times. They march after the prince of the air. Meditation on this would make us turn out of the common road.

2. Meditation on the fewness of those who shall be saved, would make us walk tremblingly. Few find the way; and when they have found it, few walk in the way. The thoughts of this would work holy fear, Heb. 4:1, not a despairing fear—but a jealous and cautious fear. This reverential fear, the eminent saints of God have had. Augustine says of himself, he knocked at heaven's gate with a trembling hand. This fear is joined with hope, Psalm 147:1. "The Lord takes pleasure in those who fear him, in those who hope in his mercy." A child of God fears, because the gate is strait; but hopes, because the gate is open.

3. Meditation on the fewness of those who shall be saved, would be a whetstone to holy industry. It would put us upon working out our salvation; if there are so few that shall be crowned, it would make us the swifter in the race. This meditation would be an alarm to sleepy Christians.

Section 9. Meditate upon Final APOSTASY.

Think what a sad thing it is to begin in religion to build, and not be able to finish. Joash was good while his uncle Jehoiada lived—but after he died, Joash grew wicked—all his religion was buried in his uncle's grave. We live in the fall of the leaf; how many are fallen to damnable heresies? 2 Pet. 2:1. Meditate seriously on that scripture, Heb. 6:4-6. "It is impossible for those who have once been enlightened, who have tasted the heavenly gift, who have shared in the Holy Spirit, who have tasted the goodness of the Word of God and the powers of the coming age, if they fall away, to be brought back to repentance." A man may be enlightened, and that from a double lamp—the Word and Spirit; but these beams, though they are irradiating, yet not penetrating. It is possible he may have a taste of the heavenly gift; he may taste but not be nourished by it. This taste may not only illuminate—but refresh; it may carry some sweetness in it, there may be a kind of delight in spiritual things. Thus far a man may go and yet fall away finally. Now this will be very sad (it being such a God-affronting, and Christ reproaching sin) "Know therefore it is an evil and bitter thing that you have forsaken the Lord," Jer. 2:19. Meditate upon final relapses.

1. Meditation on this would make us earnest in prayer to God—for soundness of heart, "Make my heart sound in your statutes," Psalm 119:80. Lord, let me not be an almost Christian. Work a thorough work of grace upon me: though I am not washed perfectly, let me be washed thoroughly, Psalm 51:2. That which begins in hypocrisy, ends in apostasy!

2. Meditation on hypocrites final falling away, would make us earnest in prayer for perseverance. "Hold up my goings in your paths that my footsteps slip not," Psalm 17:5. "Lord, hold me up that I may hold out. You have set the crown at the end of the race, let me run the race, that I may wear the crown!" It was Beza's prayer—let it be ours, "Lord perfect what you have begun in me, that I may not suffer shipwreck when I am almost at the haven."

Section 10. Meditate upon DEATH.

We say we must all die—but how rare it is—that anyone meditates seriously upon death?

1. Meditate on the certainty of death; it is appointed for all, once to die, Heb. 9:27. Death is an inviolable reality.

2. Meditate upon the proximity of death, it is near to us.We are almost setting our feet upon the dark entry of death. The poets painted time with wings; it flies—and carries us upon its wings. The race is short between the cradle and the grave! The sentence of death is already passed, Gen. 3:19. "To dust you shall return;" so that our life is but a short reprieve from death which is granted to a condemned man. "You have made my days a mere handbreadth; the span of my years is as nothing before you. Each man's life is but a breath." Psalm 39:5. Nay, our life is less than nothing, reckoned with eternity.

3. Meditate upon the uncertainty of time. We have no lease—but may be turned out the next hour; there are so many casualties, that it is a wonder if life be not cut off by untimely death. How soon may God seal us a lease of ejectment? Our grave may be dug before night. Today we may lie upon a pillow of down, tomorrow we may be laid upon a pillow of dust. Today the sermon-bell tolls, to morrow our death bell may toll.

4. Think seriously, that to die is to be but once done, and after death our state is eternally fixed. If you die in your impenitency, there is no repenting in the grave. If you leave your work at death half done, there is no finishing it in the grave, Eccl. 9:10, "There is no work, nor device, nor

wisdom in the grave where you go." If a garrison surrenders at the first summons, there is mercy. But if it battles until it is stormed and captured, there is no mercy then. Now it is a day of grace, and God holds forth the white flag of mercy to the penitent; if we battle with God until he storms us by death—there is no mercy. There is nothing to be done for our souls after death. O meditate on death. It is reported of Zeleucus, that the first piece of house-hold stuff he brought to Babylon, was a tomb-stone; think often of your tomb-stone. Meditation on death would work these admirable effects.

1. Meditation on death would pull down the plumes of pride; you are but animated dust! Shall dust and ashes be proud? You body will be turned into grass—and shall shortly be mowed down!

2. Meditation on death would be a means to give a death-wound to sin. No stronger antidote against sin, says Augustine, than the frequent meditation on death. Am I now sinning—and tomorrow I may be dying? what if death should take me doing the devil's work, would it not send me to him to receive double pay! Carry the thoughts of death as a book always about you, and when sin tempts, pull out this book, and read in it—and you shall see sin will vanish. We should look upon sin in two looking-glasses—the glass of Christ's blood, and the glass of death.

3. Meditation on death would be a bridle for intemperance; shall I pamper that body which must lie down in the house of rottenness? Our Savior at a feast breaks forth into mention of his burial, Mat. 26. Feeding upon the thoughts of death would be an excellent preservative against gluttony.

4. Meditation on death would make us use time better, and crowd up much work in a little space. Many meet in taverns to trifle away time; the apostle bids us redeem time. "Redeeming the time." Our lives should be like jewels, though little in bulk, yet great in worth. Some die young, yet with gray hairs upon them. We must be like grass of the field, useful; not like grass of the house-top, which withers before it is grown up. To live and not be serviceable, is not life—but wasting life.

5. Meditation on death would spur us on in the pursuit after holiness. Death is the great plunderer, it will shortly plunder us of all our outward comforts. Our feathers of beauty and honor must be laid in the dust—but death cannot plunder us of our graces. The commonwealth of Venice, in their armory, have this inscription, "happy is he who in time of peace, thinks of war." He who often meditates of death—will make the best preparation for it.

Section 11. Meditate on the Day of JUDGMENT.

Feathers float upon the water—but gold sinks in it. Just so, light feathery professors float in vanity, they mind not the day of judgment—but serious spirits sink deep into the meditation on it. Most men put far away from them, the evil day, Amos 3:6. They report of the Italians, that in a great thunder they use to ring the bells—that the sound of their bells may drown the noise of the thunder. Just so, the devil delights men with the music of the world, that the noise should drown the noise of the day of judgment, and make them forget the sound of the last trumpet. Most men are guilty, therefore they do not love to hear of the day of judgment. When Paul preached of judgment, Felix trembled, he had a bad conscience. Josephus tells us of Felix, that he was a wicked man—the woman that lived with him (Drusilla) he enticed away from her husband, and when he heard of judgment, he fell a trembling. Oh I beseech you meditate upon this last and solemn day; while others are thinking how they may get riches, let us bethink ourselves how we may fare on the day of judgment.

1. Meditation on the day of judgment would make us to evaluate all our actions; Christ will come with his fan and his sieve. "Will this action of mine, bide the test at that great day.

2. Meditation on the last day would make us labor to approve our hearts to God—the great judge of the world. It is no matter what men think of us—but what is our Judge's opinion of us? To him we must stand or fall. The galaxy, or milky way, as the astronomers call it, is a bright circle in the heavens containing many stars—but they are so small that they have no name, nor are they taken cognizance of by the astrologers. Give me permission to apply it; possibly others may take no notice of us; we are so small as to have no name in the world, yet if we are true stars, and can approve our hearts to God, we shall hold up our heads with boldness, when we come to stand before our Judge.

Section 12. Meditate upon HELL.

1. Meditate upon the pain of loss, Matt. 25:10, "and the door was shut." To have Christ's face veiled over, and a perpetual eclipse and midnight in the soul; to be cast out of God's presence, in whose presence is fullness of joy—this accentuates and embitters the condition of the damned. It is like mingling gall with wormwood.

2. Meditate upon the pain of sense. Psalm 9:17, "The wicked shall be turned into hell." And here meditate of two things,

1. The place of hell. 2. The company.

1. Meditate on the PLACE of hell. It is called "a place of torment," Luke 16:28. There are two things especially in hell to torment.

1. The FIRE. Rev. 20:15. It is called a lake of burning fire. Augustine, Peter Lombard, Gregory the Great, say, this fire of hell is a material fire, though they say it is infinitely hotter than any culinary fire—which is but painted fire compared to hell-fire. I wish none of us may experience what kind of fire it is! I rather think the fire of hell is partly material, and partly spiritual; the material fire is to work upon the body, the spiritual to torture the soul. This is the wrath of God, which is both fire and bellows; "who knows the power of your anger?" Psalm 90:11.

But it may be objected, if there is material fire in hell, it will consume the bodies there. I answer, It shall burn without consuming, as Moses' bush did, Exod. 3:2. The power of God silences all disputes. If God by his infinite power could make the fire not to consume the three Hebrew children; cannot he make the fire of hell burn and not consume? Augustine tells of a strange salt in Sicily, which if it be put in the fire, swims; that God who can make salt, contrary to its nature, swim in the fire—can make the bodies of the damned not consume in the fire.

2. The WORM. Mark 19:44, "Where the worm never dies." Homer in his Odyssey feigns, that Titus' liver was gnawed by two vultures in hell. This never-dying worm

Christ speaks of, is the gnawing of a guilty conscience. Melancthon calls it a hellish fury—they that will not hear conscience preaching, shall feel conscience gnawing; and so great is the extremity of these two, the fire which burns, and the worm which bites, that there will follow "gnashing of teeth," Matt. 8:12, the damned will gnash their teeth for horror and anguish. That must needs be sad fare (as Latimer says) where weeping is served for the first course, and gnashing of teeth for the second. To endure this hell will be intolerable, to escape it will be impossible!

2. Meditate of the COMPANY in hell—the devil and his demons, Matt. 25:41. Job complains he was a companion to owls, chapter 30:29. What will it be to be a companion to devils? Consider,

1. Their ghastly deformity—they make hell look blacker.

2. Their deadly antipathy—they are fired with rage against mankind. First they become tempters—then tormentors.

Meditate much on hell. Let us go into hell by contemplation—that we may not go into hell by condemnation. How restless and hopeless, is the condition of the damned! The ancients feign of Endymion, that he got permission from Jupiter always to sleep. What would the damned in hell give for such a license! In their pains is neither intermission, nor mitigation.

1. The serious meditation on hell, would make us fear sin as hell. Sin is hell's fuel! Sin like Samson's foxes, carries devouring fire in its tail.

2. Meditation on hell would cause rejoicing in a child of God. The saint's fear of hell is like the two Marys' fear, Matt. 28:8, "They departed from the sepulcher with fear and great joy." A believer may fear to think of the place of torment—but rejoice to think he shall never come into that place. When a man stands upon a high rock, he trembles to look down into the sea, yet he rejoices that he is not there struggling with the waves. A child of God, when he thinks of hell, he rejoices with trembling. A prison is not made for the king's son to be put in. A great naturalist observes that nothing will so soon quench fire as salt and blood; but I am sure of this—the salt brinish tears of repentance, and the blood of Christ will quench the fire of hell to a believer. Christ himself has felt the pains of hell for you. The Lamb of God being roasted in the fire of God's wrath—by this burnt-offering the Lord is now appeased towards his people. Oh how may the godly rejoice! "There is no condemnation to those who are in Christ!" Romans 8:1. When the Son of God was in the furnace, Dan. 3:25, the fire did no hurt the three children. Just so, Christ being for a time in the fiery furnace of God's wrath, that fire can do a believer no hurt. The saints have the garment of Christ's righteousness upon them, and the fire of hell can never singe this garment.

Section 13. Meditate upon HEAVEN.

From the mount of meditation, as from mount Nebo, we may take a view and prospect of the land of promise. Christ has taken possession of heaven in the name of all believers, Heb. 6:20, "Jesus, who went before us, has entered on our behalf." Heaven must needs be a glorious city, which has God both for its builder and inhabitant. Heaven is the extract and quintessence of all blessedness. There the saints shall have all their holy hearts can desire.

Augustine wished that he might have seen three things before he died, Rome in its glory, Paul in the pulpit, and Christ in the flesh. But the saints shall see a better sight; they shall see, not Rome—but heaven in its glory; they shall see Paul, not in the pulpit—but on the throne, and shall sit with him; they shall see Christ's flesh, not veiled over with infirmities and disgraces—but in its spiritual embroidery; not a crucified—but a glorified body. They shall "behold the king in his beauty," Isaiah 33:17.

What a glorious place will this be! In heaven "God will be all in all," 1 Cor. 15:28, beauty to the eye, music to the ears, joy to the heart; and this he will be to the poorest saint, as well as the richest. O Christian, who are now at your hard labor, perhaps following the plough—you shall sit on the throne of glory! Rev. 3:21. Quintus Curtius writes of one who was digging in his garden, and was suddenly made king, and a purple garment richly embroidered with gold put upon him. Just so shall it be done to the poorest believer—he shall be taken from his laboring work, and set at the right hand of God, having the crown of righteousness upon his head!

Meditate often on the Jerusalem above.

1. Meditation on heaven would excite and quicken OBEDIENCE. It would put spurs to our sluggish hearts, and make us "abound in the work of God, knowing that our labor is not in vain in the Lord," 1 Cor. 15:58. The weight of glory would not hinder us in our race—but cause us to run the faster! This weight would add wings to duty.

2. Meditation on heaven would make us strive after heart PURITY, because only the "pure in heart shall see

God," Matt. 5:8. It is only a clear eye which can look on a bright transparent object.

3. Meditation on heaven would be a pillar of SUPPORT under our sufferings. Heaven will make amends for all. One hour in heaven will make us forget all our sorrows! The sun dries up the water; just so—one beam of God's glorious face will dry up all our tears.

Section 14. Meditate on ETERNITY.

Millions of years stand only for ciphers in eternity, and signify nothing. What an amazing word is eternity! Eternity to the godly--is a day which has no sun-setting! Eternity to the wicked--is a night which has no sun-rising! Eternity is a gulf which may swallow up all our thoughts: Meditate on that scripture, "And they will go away into eternal punishment, but the righteous will go into eternal life." Matthew 25:46.

1. Meditate upon eternal PUNISHMENT. The bitter cup the damned drink of, shall never pass away from them. The sinner and the furnace shall never be parted. God's vial of wrath will be always dropping upon a wicked man. When you have reckoned up so many myriads and millions of years, nay, ages—as have passed the bounds of all arithmetic, eternity is not yet begun! This word forever breaks the heart! If the tree falls hell-ward—there it lies to all eternity! Now is the time of God's long-suffering, after death will be the time of the sinner's long-suffering, when he shall "suffer the vengeance of eternal fire!" Jude 7.

2. Meditate upon eternal LIFE. The soul that is once landed at the heavenly shore, is past all storms. The glorified soul shall be forever bathing itself in the rivers of

pleasure. "You have made known to me the path of life; you will fill me with joy in your presence, with eternal pleasures at your right hand." Psalms 16:11. This is what makes heaven to be heaven—"We shall be forever with the Lord!" 1 Thess. 4:17. Augustine says, "Lord, I am content to suffer any pains and torments in this world—if I might see your face one day. But alas, were it only a day, then to be ejected from heaven—it would rather be an aggravation of misery!" But this word, "forever with the Lord," makes up the garland of glory! A state of eternity, is a state of security.

1. Meditation on eternity, would make us very SERIOUS in what we do. Zeuxes being asked, why he took so long to paint a picture, answered, "I paint for eternity." The thoughts of an irreversible condition after this life, would make us pray and live as for eternity.

2. Meditation on eternity, would make us overlook present WORLDLY things—as flitting and fading. What is this present world, to him who has eternity in his eye? it is but nothing. He who thinks of eternity will despise "the passing pleasures of sin."

3. Meditation on eternity would be a means to keep us from envying the wicked's prosperity. Here the wicked may be "dressed in purple and fine linen, and live in luxury every day." But what is this, compared to eternity? As long as there is such a thing as eternity, God has time enough to reckon with all his enemies!

Section 15. Meditate upon your EXPERIENCES.

The last subject of meditation is your experiences. Look over your receipts:

1. Has not God provided liberally for you, and given you those spiritual mercies, which he has denied to others who are better than you? Here is an experience, Gen: 48:15. "The God who has fed me all my days." You never eat—but mercy carves for you. You never go to bed—but mercy draws the curtain, and sets a guard of angels about you. Whatever you have, is out of the treasury of free grace! Here is an experience to meditate upon.

2. Has not God prevented many dangers—has he not kept watch and ward about you?

1. What temporal dangers has God screened off? Your neighbor's house on fire—but it has not kindled in your dwellings. Another is infected with the plague—but you are healthy. Behold the golden feathers of protection covering you!

2. What spiritual dangers has God prevented? when others have been poisoned with error, you have been preserved. God has sounded a retreat to you; you have heard "a voice behind you saying—This is the way, walk in it!" When you had enlisted yourself, and taken pay on the devil's side—yet God has "plucked you as a brand out of the fire," turned your heart, and now you espouse Christ's quarrel against sin. Behold preventing grace! Here is an experience to meditate upon.

3. Has not God spared you a long time? Why is it, that others are struck dead in the act of sin—as Ananias and Sapphira—and you are preserved as a monument of God's patience?

Here is an experience: God has done more for you than for the fallen angels; he never granted them repentance—but he has waited for you year after year, Isaiah 30:18. Therefore "will the Lord wait that he may be gracious." He has not only knocked at your heart in the ministry of the word—but he has waited at the door. How long has his Spirit striven with you; like an importunate suitor, who after many denials, yet will not give over the suit. Methinks I see JUSTICE with a sword in its hand ready to strike! But MERCY steps in for the sinner, "Lord, have patience with him a while longer!" Methinks I hear the angels say to God, as the king of Israel once said to the prophet Elisha, 2 Kings 6:22, "Shall I smite them? shall I smite them?" Methinks I hear the angels say, "Shall we take off the head of such a drunkard, swearer, blasphemer?" But MERCY seems to answer as the vine-dresser, Luke 13:8, "Let him alone this year," see if he will repent. Is not here an experience worth meditating upon? Mercy turns justice into a rainbow; the rainbow is a bow indeed—but has no arrow in it! That justice has been like the rainbow without an arrow—that it has not shot you to death—here is a monument of patience to read over and meditate upon.

4. Has not God often come in with assisting grace? When he has bid you mortify such a lust, and you have said as Jehoshaphat, 2 Chron. 20:12, "I have no might against this great army!" Then God has come in with auxiliary force, and "his grace has been sufficient." When God has bid you pray for such a mercy, and you have found yourself very unfit; your heart was at first dead and flat, all of a sudden you are carried above your own strength; your tears drop, and your love flames! God has come in with assisting grace. If the heart burns in prayer—God has struck the fire! The Spirit has been tuning your soul, and now you make sweet melody in prayer. Here is an experience to meditate upon.

5. Has not God vanquished Satan for you? When the devil has tempted to infidelity, to self-murder, when he would make you believe either that your graces were but a fiction, or God's promise but a counterfeit bond; yet you have not been foiled by the tempter—it is God who has kept the garrison of your heart, else Satan's fiery darts would have entered! Here is an experience to meditate on.

6. Have you not had many signal deliverances? When you have been even at the gates of death, God has miraculously recovered you, and renewed your strength as the eagle! May not you write that writing which Hezekiah did? Isaiah 38:6, "The writing of Hezekiah King of Judah, when he had been sick, and was recovered of his sickness." You thought the sun of your life was quite setting—but God made this sun turn back many degrees. Here is an experience for meditation to feed upon.

When you have been imprisoned by sin—your foot taken in the snare, and the Lord has broken the snare, nay, has made those to break it, who were the instruments of laying it—behold an experience to meditate on! Oh let us often revolve in mind, our experiences. You who have rare receipts of mercy—be often by meditation, looking over your receipts.

1. Meditation on our experiences would raise us to THANKFULNESS. Considering that God has set a hedge of providence about us—he has strewed our way with roses—this would make us take the harp and violin—and praise the Lord, (1 Chron. 16:4). And not only praise—but record our blessings. The meditating Christian keeps a register or chronicle of God's mercies, that their memory does not decay. God would have the manna kept in the ark

many hundred years, that the remembrance of that miracle might be preserved; a meditating soul takes care that the spiritual manna of an experience be kept safe.

2. Meditation on our experiences would engage our hearts to God in OBEDIENCE. Mercy would be a needle to sew us to him! We would cry out as Bernard, "I have, Lord, two mites—a soul and a body—and I give them both to you."

3. Meditation on our experiences would serve to convince us that GOD is no hard master. We might bring in our experiences as a sufficient confutation of that slander. When we have been falling—has not God taken us by the hand? "When I said, 'My foot is slipping,' your love, O Lord, supported me!" Psalm 94:18. How often has God supported our head and heart—when we have been fainting? And is he a hard Master? Is there any Master besides God—who will wait upon his servants? Christians, summon in your experiences. What spiritual enjoyments have you had? What inward serenity and peace—which neither the world can give, nor death take away! A Christian's own experiences may plead for God—against those who desire to censure his ways rather than to try them; and to cavil at them, rather than to walk in them.

4. Meditation on our experiences would make us communicative to others. We would be willing to tell our children and acquaintances, what God has done for our souls— At such a time we were brought low, and God raised us; at such a time in desertion, and God brought a promise to remembrance which dropped in comfort. Meditation on God's gracious dealing with us, would make us transmit and propagate our experience to others, that the

mercies of God shown to us, may bear a plentiful crop of praise when we are dead and gone!

So much for the subject matter of meditation; I proceed next to the necessity of meditation.

VII. Showing the NECESSITY of Meditation.

It is not enough to carry 'God's book' about us—but we must meditate on it. The necessity of meditation will appear in three particulars.

1. The end why God has given us his Word written and preached, is not only to know it—but that we should meditate in it. The Scripture is a love letter which the great God has written to us. We must not run it over in haste—but meditate upon God's wisdom in writing, and his love in sending it to us. Why does the physician give his patient a remedy; is it only that he should read it over and know the remedy—or that he should apply it? The end why God communicates his gospel remedies to us, is, that we should apply them by fruitful meditation. Do you think that God would ever have been at the pains of writing his law with his own finger—only that we should have the theory and notion of it? Is it not that we should meditate on it? Would he ever have been at the cost to send abroad his ministers into the world, to furnish them with gifts, Eph. 4, and must they for the work of Christ be near unto death—that the Christians should only have an empty head knowledge of the truths published? Is it speculation or meditation—which God aims at?

2. The necessity of meditation appears in this, because without it we can never be godly Christians. A Christian

without meditation is like a soldier without weapons, or a workman without tools.

Without meditation, the truths of God will not stay with us. The heart is hard, and the memory slippery—and without meditation all is lost! Meditation imprints and fastens a truth in the mind. Serious meditation is like the engraving of letters in gold or marble which endures. Without meditation, all our preaching is but like writing in sand, or like pouring water into a sieve. Reading and hearing without meditation, is like weak medicine which will not work. Lack of meditation has made so many sermons in this age, to have a miscarrying womb and dry breasts!

3. Without meditation the truths which we know will never affect our hearts. Deut. 6:6, "These words which I command this day shall be in your heart." How can the Word be in the heart—unless it be wrought in by meditation? As an hammer drives a nail to the head—so meditation drives a truth to the heart. It is not the taking in of food—but the stomach's digesting it, which makes it turn into nourishment. Just so, it is not the taking in of a truth at the ear—but the meditating on it, which is the digestion of it in the mind, which makes it nourish. Without meditation, the Word preached may increase notion, but not affection. There is as much difference between the knowledge of a truth, and the meditation on a truth, as there is between the light of a torch, and the light of the sun. Set up a lamp or torch in the garden, and it has no influence. But the sun has a sweet influence, it makes the plants to grow, and the herbs to flourish. Just so, knowledge is like a torch lighted in the understanding, which has little or no influence—it does not make not a man the better. But meditation is like the shining of the sun—it operates upon the affections, it

warms the heart and makes it more holy. Meditation fetches life in a truth. There are many truths which lie, as it were, in the heart dead—which when we meditate upon, they begin to have life and heat in them. Meditation on a truth is like rubbing a man in a swoon—it fetches life. It is meditation, which makes a Christian!

4. Without meditation we make ourselves guilty of slighting God and his Word. If a man lets a thing lie aside, and never minds it—it is a sign he slights it. God's Word is the book of life; not to meditate in it—is to undervalue it. If a king puts forth an edict or proclamation, and the subjects never mind it—it is a slighting of the king's authority. God puts forth his law as a royal edict; if we do not meditate on it, it is a slighting his authority, and contempt done to the divine majesty!

VIII. Showing the reason WHY there are so few godly Christians.

Use 1. Information.

It gives us a true account why there are so few godly Christians in the world; namely, because there are so few meditating Christians. We have many who have Bible ears, they are swift to hear—but slow to meditate. This duty is grown almost out of fashion, people are so much in the shop, that they are seldom on the Mount with God. Where is the meditating Christian? Where is he who meditates on sin, hell, eternity, the recompense of reward—who takes a prospect of heaven every day? Where is the meditating Christian? It is to be bewailed in our times, that so many who go under the name of professors, have banished godly discourse from their tables, and meditation from their closets. Surely the hand of Joab is in this.

The devil is an enemy to meditation; he cares not how much people read and hear; he knows that meditation is a means to compose the heart, and bring it into a gracious frame. Satan is content that you should be hearing and praying Christians, just so long as you are not meditating Christians. He can stand your small shot, provided you do not put in this bullet.

IX. A REPROOF to such as do not Meditate in God's Word.

Use 2. Of reproof.

It serves to reprove those who meditate indeed—but not in the Word of God. They turn all their meditations the wrong way; like a man who lets forth the water of his mill which should grind his corn, into the highway, where it does no good. Just so, there are many who let out their meditations upon other fruitless things which are in no way beneficial to their souls.

1. The farmer meditates on his acres of land, not upon his soul. His meditation is how he may improve a barren piece of ground, not how he may improve a barren mind; he will not let his ground lie fallow—but he lets his heart lie fallow; there is no spiritual culture, not one seed of grace sown there.

2. The physician meditates upon his remedies—but seldom on those remedies which the gospel prescribes for his salvation, faith and repentance. Commonly the devil is

physician to the physician, having given him such stupefying drug, that for the most part he dies of a lethargy.

3. The lawyer meditates upon the common law; but as for God's law he seldom meditates in it either day or night. The lawyer while he is meditating on his client's evidences, often forgets his own; most have their spiritual evidences to seek, when they should have them to show.

4. The tradesman is for the most part meditating upon his wares; his study is how he may increase his estate, and make the ten talents into a hundred. He is "cumbered about many things;" he does not meditate in the book of God's book—but in his account-book day and night. In the long run you will see these were fruitless meditations, you will find that you are but golden beggars, and have gotten but the fool's purchase when you die, Luke 12:20.

5. There is another sort that meditate only upon mischief, "who devise iniquity," Mic. 2:1. They meditate how to defame and to defraud; Amos 8:5, "They make the ephah small, and the shekel great." The ephah was a measure used in buying, the shekel a weight used in selling. Many who should support, too often supplant one another. And how many meditate revenge? It is sweet to them as dropping honey. "Their hearts shall meditate terror," Isaiah 38:18. The sinner is a felon to himself, and God will make him a terror to himself.

X. A holy PERSUASIVE to Meditation.

Use 3. Of Exhortation.

I am in the next place to exhort Christians to this so necessary duty of meditation. If ever there were a duty I would press upon you with more earnestness and zeal, it would be this, because so much of the vitals and spirit of religion lies in it. The plant may as well bear fruit without watering, the food may as well nourish without digesting, as we can fructify in holiness without meditation. God provides the food, ministers can but cook and dress it for you—but it must be inwardly digested by meditation. For lack of this you may cry out with the prophet, Isaiah 24:16, "My leanness, my leanness, woe unto me." O let me persuade such as fear God, seriously to set upon this duty. If you have formerly neglected it, bewail your neglect, and now begin to make conscience of it! Lock up yourselves with God (at least once a day) by holy meditation. Ascend this hill, and when you have gotten to the top of it—you shall see a fair prospect—Christ and heaven before you. Let me put you in mind of that saying of Bernard, "O saint, know you not that your husband Christ is bashful, and will not be affectionate in company, retire yourself by meditation into the closet, or the field, and there you shall have Christ's embraces." Cant. 7:11, 12, "Come, my beloved, let us go forth into the field, there will I give you my love."

O that I might invite Christians to this rare duty. Why is it that you do not meditate in God's law? Let me expostulate the case with you; what is the reason? Methinks I hear some say, "We are indeed convinced of the necessity of the duty—but alas there are many things that hinder!" There are two great objections that lie in the way, I shall remove them, and then hope the better to persuade to this duty.

XI. The answering of OBJECTIONS.

Objection 1. I have so much business in the world, that I have no time to meditate.

Answer. The world indeed is a great enemy to meditation. It is easy to lose one's purse in a crowd; and in a crowd of worldly employments, it is easy to lose all the thoughts of God. So long as the heart is an Exchange, I do not expect that it should be a Temple. But, to answer the objection; have you so much business that you have no time for meditation—as if piety were a minor matter—a thing fit only for idle hours? What! No time to meditate! What is the business of your life—but meditation? God never sent us into the world to get riches, (I speak not against labor in a vocation) but I say this is not the end of our existence. The errand God sent us into the world about, is salvation; and that we may attain the end, we must use the means, namely, holy meditation. Now, have you no time to meditate? just as if a farmer should say that he has so much business, that he has no time to plough or sow; why, what is his occupation but plowing and sowing!

What a madness is it to hear Christians say they have no time to meditate? what is the business of their lives but meditation? O take heed lest by growing rich, you grow worth nothing at last. Take heed that God does not sue out the statute of bankruptcy against you, and you be disgraced before men and angels. No time for meditation! You shall observe that others in former ages have had as much business as you, and public affairs to look after, yet they were called upon to meditate, Josh. 1:8. "You shall meditate in this book of the Law." Joshua might have pleaded an excuse, he was a soldier, a commander, and the care of marshaling his army lay chiefly upon him, yet this must not take him off from piety; Joshua must meditate in the book of God's law. God never intended that the great business of piety should give way to a shop or farm; or that a particular vocation should jostle out the general duty to holiness.

2. Objection. But this duty of meditation is hard. To set time apart every day to get the heart into a meditating frame is very difficult; Gerson reports of himself, that he was sometimes three or four hours before he could work his heart into a spiritual frame.

Answer. Does this hinder? To this I shall give a threefold reply.

1. The price that God has set heaven at, is labor. Our salvation cost Christ blood, it may well cost us sweat. "The kingdom of heaven suffers violence," Matt. 11:12. It is as a garrison which holds out, and the duties of religion are the taking it by storm. A godly Christian must offer violence to himself, (though not natural-self, yet sinful-self.) Self is nothing but the flesh. The flesh cries out for ease, it is a libertine! It is reluctant to take pains, reluctant to pray, to repent—it is reluctant to put its neck under Christ's yoke! Now a Christian must hate himself; no man ever yet hated his own flesh, Eph. 5:29. Yes, in this sense he must hate his own flesh, "The lusts of the flesh," Romans 8:13. He must offer violence to himself by mortification and meditation. You say that it is hard to meditate. Is it not harder to lie in hell?

2. We do not argue so in other things; riches are hard to come by, therefore I will sit still and be without them. No! Difficulty is the whetstone of industry. How will men venture for gold? and shall we not spend and be spent for that which is more precious than the gold of Ophir? By meditation we suck out the quintessence of a promise.

3. Though while we are first entering upon meditation it may seem hard, yet when once we are entered it is sweet and pleasant. Christ's yoke at the first putting on, may seem heavy—but when once it is on, it becomes easy; it is not a yoke, but a crown. "Lord," says Austin, "the more I meditate on you, the sweeter you are to me!" According to holy David, "My meditation on you shall be sweet," Psalm 104:34. The poets say the top of Olympus was always quiet and serene. Just so, it is hard climbing up the rocky hill of meditation—but when we are got up to the top, there is a pleasant prospect, and we shall sometimes think ourselves even in heaven. By holy meditation the soul does as it were, breakfast with God every morning. When a Christian is upon the mount of meditation, he is like Peter on the mount when Christ was transfigured, Matt. 17. He cries out, "Lord, it is good to be here!" He is reluctant to go down the mount again. If you come to him, and tell him of a purchase, he thinks you bid him to his loss!

What hidden manna does the soul taste, now that it is on the mount! How sweet are the visits of God's Spirit! When Christ was alone in the wilderness, then the angel came to comfort him. When the soul is alone in holy meditation and prayer, then not an angel—but God's own Spirit does come to comfort him. A Christian who meets with God in the mount, would not exchange his hours of meditation for the most orient pearls or sparkling beauties that the world can afford. No wonder David spent the whole day in meditation, Psalm 119:97. Nay, as if the day had been too little, he borrows a part of the night too, Psalm 63:6, "when I remember you upon my bed, and meditate on you in the night watches." When others were sleeping, David was meditating. He who is given much to meditation, shall with Sampson find a honeycomb in this duty. Therefore let not the difficulty, discourage. The pleasantness will infinitely countervail the pains.

XII. Concerning OCCASIONAL Meditations.

Having removed these two objections out of the way, let me again revive the exhortation to "meditate in God's law day and night." And there are two sorts of meditation which I would persuade to—

1. Occasional, and 2. Deliberate.

1. OCCASIONAL meditations, such as are taken up on any sudden occasion. There is nothing almost which occurs—but we may presently raise some meditation upon. As a good herbalist extracts the spirits and quintessence out of every herb, so a Christian may extract matter of meditation, from every occurrence. A gracious heart, like fire, turns all objects into fuel for meditation. I shall give you some instances. When you look up to the heavens, and see them richly embroidered with light, you may raise this meditation. If the footstool is so glorious, what is the throne where God himself sits! When you see the skies bespangled with stars, think, what is Christ The Bright Morning Star! Monica, Augustine's mother, standing one day, and seeing the sun shine, raised this meditation, "Oh! if the sun is so bright, what is the light of God's presence?" When you hear music which delights the senses, presently raise this

meditation, "What music like a good conscience; this is the bird of paradise within, whose chirping melody does enchant and ravish the soul with joy!" He who has this music all day, may take David's pillow at night, and say with that sweet singer, "I will lay me down in peace and sleep," Psalm. 4:8. How blessed is he who can find heaven in his own bosom!

When you are dressing yourselves in the morning, awaken your meditation, think thus—but have I been dressing the hidden man of the heart? Have I looked at my heart in the glass of God's Word? I have put on my clothes—but have I put on Christ? it is reported of Pambo, that seeing a gentlewoman dressing herself all the morning by her glass, he fell a-weeping: "O says he, this woman has spent the morning in dressing her body, and I sometimes spend scarcely an hour in dressing my soul!" When you sit down to dinner, let your meditation feed upon this first course, "How blessed are those who shall eat bread in the kingdom of God! What a royal feast will that be, which God prepares! What a love-feast will that be, where none shall be admitted but friends!"

When you go to bed at night, imagine thus, "Shortly I shall put off the earthly clothes of my body, and make my bed in the grave!" When you see the judge going to court, and hear the trumpet blow, think with yourselves, as Hierom did, that you are still hearing that shrill trumpet sounding in your ears, "Arise you dead and come to judgment!" When you see a poor man going on the streets, raise this meditation, "Here is a walking picture of Christ!" He had no place where to lay his head, Matt. 8:10. My Savior became poor, that I through his poverty might be made rich!" When you go to church, think thus, "I am now going to hear God speak, let me not stop my ear; if I refuse to hear him speaking in his Word, I shall next hear him speaking in his wrath!" Psalm 2:5.

When you walk abroad in your orchard, and see the plants bearing, and the herbs nourishing, think how pleasing a sight it is to God—to see a thriving Christian; how beautiful are the trees of righteousness when they are hung full of fruit—when they abound in faith, humility, knowledge! When you pluck a rose-bud in your gardens, raise this contemplation, "How lovely are the early buddings of grace! God prizes a Christian in the bud, he likes the blooming of youth, rather than the shedding of old age!" When you eat a grape from the tree, think of Christ the true vine; how precious is the blood of that grape! such rare clusters grow there, that the angels themselves delight to taste of!

It is said of Augustine, he was much in these extempore meditations. A gracious heart, like the philosopher's magic stone, turns all into gold—he has heavenly meditations from earthly occurrences. The skilled chemist, when several metals are mingled together, can by his skill extract the gold and silver from the baser metals. Just so, a Christian, by a divine chemistry, can extract golden meditations from the various earthly objects he beholds! Indeed it argues a spiritual heart, to turn everything to a spiritual use; and we have Christ's own example for these occasional meditations, John 4:7-14. While he sat on Jacob's well, he presently meditates on that, and breaks forth into a most excellent discourse concerning the water of life. So much for occasional meditations.

2. Be exhorted to DELIBERATE meditations, which are the chief. Set some time apart every day, that you may

in a serious and solemn manner converse with God in the mount: A godly man, is a man set apart, Psalm 4:3, as God sets him apart by election, so he sets him apart by meditation.

XIII. The fittest TIME for Meditation.

Question 1. What is the fittest time for meditation?

Answer. For the timing of it, it is rather hard to prescribe, because of men's various callings and employments. But if I may freely speak my thoughts, the morning is the fittest time for meditation. The best time to converse with God is, when we may be most in private, that is, before worldly concerns stand knocking as so many suitors at the door to be let in. The morning is, as it were, the cream of the day—let the cream be taken off, and let God have it. In the distilling of strong-water, the first water that is drawn from the still is more full of spirits, the second drawing is weaker; so the first meditations that are stilled from the mind in a morning, are the best, and we shall find them to be most full of life and spirits. The morning is the golden hour. God loved the first-fruits, Exod. 23:19. "The first of the first-fruits you shall bring into the house of the Lord." Let God have the first-fruits of the day; the first of our thoughts must be reserved for heaven. The student takes the morning for his study. The usurer gets up in the morning and looks over his books of account: a Christian must begin with God in the morning. David was with God before break of day, Psalm 119:147. "I rise before dawn and cry out for help; I put my hope in Your Word."

Question 2. But why the morning for meditation?

Answer 1. Because in the morning the mind is fittest for holy duties; a Christian is most himself then. What weary devotion will there be at night when a man is even tired out with the business of the day! He will be fitter to sleep, than to meditate. The morning is the queen of the day; then the imagination is quickest, the memory strongest, the spirits freshest, the body most refreshed, having restored its strength by sleep. It is a sure rule, then is the best time to serve God, when we find ourselves most in tune. In the morning the heart is like a violin—strung and put in tune, and then it makes the sweetest melody.

2. The morning thoughts stay longest with us the whole day afterwards. The wool takes the first dye best, and is not easily worn out. When the mind receives the impression of good thoughts in the morning, it holds this sacred dye the better; and like an ingrained color, it will not easily be lost. The heart keeps the relish of morning meditations, as a cup receives a tincture and savor of the wine which is first put into it; or as linen in a cedar chest—which keeps the scent a great while after. Perfume your mind with heavenly thoughts in the morning—and it will not lose its spiritual fragrancy! Wind up your heart towards heaven in the beginning of the day—and it will go the better all the day afterwards. It is with receiving thoughts into the mind, as it is with receiving guests into an inn—the first guests which come, will get the best rooms in the house; if others come afterwards, they get the worse rooms. Just so, when the mind entertains holy meditations for its morning-guests, if afterwards earthly thoughts come, they are put into some of the worst rooms—they lodge lowest in the affections. The best rooms are taken up in the morning,

for Christ. He who loses his heart in the morning, in the world; will hardly find it again all the day after.

3. It is a part of that solemn respect and honor we give to God—to let him have the first thoughts of the day. We give people of quality, the best treatment—we let them take the first place. If we honor God (whose name is reverend and holy) we will let the thoughts of God take first place. When the world has the first of our thoughts, it is a sign the world lies uppermost, we love it most. The first thing a covetous man meditates on in the morning, is his money; a sign his gold lies nearest to his heart. O! Christians, let God have your morning meditations. He takes it in disdain, to have the world served before him. Suppose a king and a criminal were to dine in the same room, and to sit at two tables; if the criminal would have his food brought up, and be served first, the king might take it in high disdain, and look upon it as a contempt done to his person. When the world is served first, all our morning thoughts attending it; and the Lord shall be put off with the dregs of the day, when our thoughts begin to run low—is not this a contempt done to the God of glory!

4. Equity requires it. God deserves the first of our thoughts; some of his first thoughts were upon us; we had a being in his thoughts; before we had a being he thought upon us, Eph. 1:4. "Before the foundations of the world." Before we fell, he was thinking how to raise us. We had the morning of his thoughts. O! what thoughts of free grace, what thoughts of peace has he had towards us! We have taken up his thoughts from eternity; if we have had some of God's first thoughts, well may he have our first thoughts.

5. This is to imitate the pattern of the saints. Job rose early in the morning, and offered sacrifice, Job 1:5. David,

when he awaked, was with God, Psalm 139:17, and indeed this is the way to have a morning blessing. "In the morning the dew fell," Exod. 16:13. The dew of a blessing falls early—now we are likeliest to have God's company. If you would meet with a friend, you go early in the morning before he be gone out. We read that the Holy Spirit came down upon the apostles, Acts 2:3, 4, and it was in the morning, as may be gathered from Peter's sermon, verse 15, it was but "the third hour of the day." The morning is the time for fruitfulness, "In the morning shall you make your seed to flourish," Isaiah 17:11. By morning meditation, we make the seed of grace to flourish.

I would not by this, wholly exclude EVENING meditation. Isaac went out to meditate in the eventide, Gen. 24:63. When business is over, and everything calm, it is good to take a turn with God in the evening. God had his evening sacrifice, as well as his morning, Ex. 29:39. As the cream at the top is sweet, so is the sugar at the bottom; in two cases, the evening meditation does well.

1. In case such has been the urgency of business, that you have time only for reading and prayer; then recompense the lack of the morning meditation, with evening meditation.

2. In case you find yourself more inclinable to good thoughts in the evening, for sometimes there is a greater impetus upon the heart, a greater aptitude and tuneableness of mind, dare not neglect meditation at such a time. Who knows but it may be a quenching the Spirit; do not drive this blessed dove from the ark of your soul. In these cases evening meditation is seasonable. But I say, if I may cast in my verdict, the morning is to be preferred; as the flower of the sun opens in the morning to take in the sweet beams of

the sun, so open your soul in the morning to take in the sweet thoughts of God. So much for the timing of meditation.

XIV. How LONG Christians should meditate.

Question 2. But how long should I meditate?

Answer. If we consider how long the world has, it is fit that we give God at least one half hour every day. I shall only say this for a general rule—meditate so long until you find your heart grow warm in this duty.

If when a man is cold, you ask how long he should stand by the fire? Surely, until he be thoroughly warm, and made fit for his work. So, Christian, your heart is cold; never a day, no not the hottest day in summer—but your heart freezes; now stand at the fire of meditation until you find your affections warmed, and you are made fit for spiritual service. David mused until his heart waxed hot within him, Psalm 39:3. I will conclude this with that excellent saying of Bernard, "Lord, I will never come away from you—without you." Let this be a Christian's resolution—not to leave off his meditations of God until he finds something of God in him—some "moving of affections after God," Cant. 5:4. Some "flamings of love," Cant. 6:8.

XV. Concerning the USEFULNESS of Meditation.

Having answered these questions, I shall next show the benefit and usefulness of meditation. I know not any duty that brings in greater income and revenue than this. It is reported of Thales, that he left the affairs of state to become a contemplating philosopher. O! did we know the advantage which comes by this duty, we would often retire from the noise and hurry of the world, that we might give ourselves to meditation.

The benefit of meditation appears in seven particulars.

1. Meditation is an excellent means to profit by the Word. Reading may bring a truth into the head, meditation brings it into the heart! It is better to meditate on one sermon—than to hear five sermons. Many complain that they do not profit from sermons; this may be the chief reason—because they chew not the cud—they do not meditate on what they have heard. If an angel should come from heaven, and preach to men, nay, if Jesus Christ himself were their preacher, they would never profit without meditation. It is the settling of the milk that makes it turn to cream; and it is the settling of a truth in the mind, that makes it turn to spiritual nourishment. The bee sucks the flower, and then works it in the hive, and makes honey of it. The hearing of a truth preached is the sucking of a flower, there must be a working it in the hive of the heart by meditation, then it turns to honey. There is a disease in children called the rickets, when they have large heads—but their lower parts are small and thrive not. Many professors have the spiritual rickets, they have large heads, much knowledge—but yet they thrive not in godliness, their heart is faint, their feet feeble, they don't walk vigorously in the ways of God; and the cause of this disease is, the lack of meditation. Bible knowledge without meditation, makes us no better than devils! Satan is an angel of light, yet black enough.

2. Meditation makes the heart serious, and then it is ever best. Meditation ballasts the heart; when the ship is ballasted, it is not so soon overturned by the wind; and when the heart is ballasted with meditation, it is not so soon overturned with vanity. Some Christians have light hearts, Zeph. 3:4, "his prophets are light." A light Christian will be blown into any opinion or vice; you may blow a feather any way: there are many feathery Christians; the devil no sooner comes with a temptation but they are ready to take fire. But meditation makes the heart serious, and God says of a serious Christian, as David of Goliath's sword, "there is none like that, give it to me." Meditation consolidates a Christian; solid gold is best; the solid Christian is the only metal that will pass current with God. The more serious the heart grows, the more spiritual, and the more spiritual, the more it resembles the Father of spirits. When a man is serious he is fittest for employment. The serious Christian is fittest for service, and it is meditation which brings the heart into this blessed frame.

3. Meditation is the bellows of the affections. Meditation hatches good affections, as the hen hatches her young ones by sitting on them. We light affection at this fire of meditation, "while I was musing the fire burned," Psalm 39:3. David was meditating on mortality, and see how his heart was affected with it, verse 4, "Lord, remind me how brief my time on earth will be. Remind me that my days are numbered, and that my life is fleeing away." The reason our affections are so chill and cold in spiritual things, is, because we do not warm ourselves more at the fire of meditation. Illumination makes us shining lamps, meditation makes us burning lamps. What is it to know Christ by speculation, and not by affection? It is the proper work of meditation to excite and blow up holy affections. What sparkling of love in such a soul! When David had

meditated on God's law, he could not choose it, but love it, Psalm 119:97. "O how love I your law! it is my meditation all the day." When the spouse had by meditation viewed those singular beauties in her beloved, white and ruddy, Cant. 5. she grew lovesick, verse 8. Galeatius Caraccialus, that famous Marquis of Vico, who had been much in the contemplation of Christ, breaks out into a holy pathos, "Let their money perish with them, who esteem all the gold in the world worth one hour's communion with Jesus Christ!"

4. Meditation fits for holy duties. The musician first puts his instrument in tune—and then he plays a song. Just so, meditation tunes the heart—and then it is fit for any holy service. As the sails to the ship, so is meditation to duty, it carries on the soul more swiftly.

1. Meditation fits for HEARING. When the ground is softened by meditation, now is a fit time for the seed of the Word to be sown.

2. Meditation fits for PRAYER. Prayer is the spiritual pulse of the soul, by which it beats strongly after God. There is no living without prayer; a man cannot live—unless he breathes; no more can the soul live—unless it breathes out its desires to God. Prayer ushers in mercy, and prayer sanctifies mercy, it makes mercy to be mercy, 1 Tim. 4:5. Prayer has power over God, Hos. 12:4. Prayer comes with letters of request to heaven. Prayer is the spiritual leech—which sucks the poison of sin out of the soul. What a blessed (shall I say duty or) privilege is prayer! Meditation is a help to prayer; Gerson calls it the nurse of prayer. Meditation is like oil to the lamp; the lamp of prayer will soon go out unless meditation feeds it. Meditation and prayer are like two turtles-doves—if you separate one, the other dies. A skillful angler observes the

time and season when the fish bite best, and then he throws in his hook. Just so, when the heart is warmed by meditation, now is the best season to throw in the hook of prayer, and fish for mercy. After Isaac had been in the field meditating, he was fit for prayer when he came home. When the gun is full of powder, it is fittest to discharge. So when the mind is full of good thoughts, a Christian is fittest by prayer to discharge, now he sends up whole volleys of sighs and groans to heaven.

Meditation has a double benefit in it—it pours in, and pours out. First it pours good thoughts into the mind, and then it pours out those thoughts again into prayer. Meditation first furnishes with matter to pray, and then it furnishes with a heart to pray, Psalm 39:3. "I was musing," says David, and the very next words are a prayer, "Lord make me to know my end;" and Psalm 143:5, 6, "I muse on the works of your hands, I stretch forth my hands to you;" the musing of his head made way for the stretching forth of his hands in prayer. When Christ was upon the mount, then he prayed. Just so, when the soul is upon the mount of meditation, now it is in tune for prayer. Prayer is the child of meditation. Meditation leads the van, and prayer brings up the rear.

3. Meditation fits for HUMILIATION. When David had been contemplating the works of creation, their splendor, harmony, motion, influence—the plumes of pride fall off—and he begins to have self-abasing thoughts, Psalm 8:3, 4. "When I consider the heavens, the work of your fingers, the moon and stars which you have ordained—What is man that you are mindful of him!"

4. Meditation is a strong antidote against SIN. Most sin is committed for lack of meditation. Men often sin

through ignorance. Would they be so brutishly sensual as they are, if they did seriously meditate upon what sin is? Would they take this viper in their hand—if they did but consider its sting? Sin puts a worm into conscience, a sting into death, and a fire into hell. Did men meditate on this—that after all their dainty dishes, death will bring in the reckoning, and they must pay the reckoning in hell—they would say as David in another sense, "let me not eat of their dainties," Psalm 141:4. The devil's apple has a bitter core in it. Did men think of this—surely it would put them into a cold sweat, and be as the angel's drawn sword to affright them! Meditation is a golden shield to beat back sin! When Joseph's mistress tempted him to wickedness, meditation did preserve him, "How can I do this great wickedness and sin against God?" Meditation makes the heart like wet tinder—it will not take the devil's fire!

5. Meditation is a cure of COVETOUSNESS. The covetous man is an idolater, Col. 3:5. Though he will not bow down to an idol, yet he worships engraved images in his coins. Now meditation is an excellent means to lessen our esteem of the world. Great things seem little to him who stands high; if he could live among the stars—the earth would seem as nothing. To a Christian who stands high upon the pinnacle of meditation—how do all worldly things disappear, and seem as nothing to him! He does not see in them, what men of the world see. He is gotten into his tower, and heaven is his prospect. What is said of God, "He dwells on high, he humbles himself to behold the things done on the earth," Psalm 113:6, I may allude to with reverence. The Christian who dwells on high by meditation, accounts it an abasing of himself, to look down upon the earth, and behold the things done in this lower region. Paul, whose meditations were sublime and seraphic, looked at things which were not seen, 2 Cor. 4 ult. How did

he trample upon the world, how did he scorn it? "I am crucified to the world," Gal. 6:14, as if he had said, "it is too much below me, to mind it!" He who is catching at a crown, will not fish for minnows. A Christian who is elevated by holy meditation, will not set his heart where his feet should be—upon the earth.

6. Holy meditation banishes vain and sinful thoughts. It purges the imagination, "How long shall vain thoughts lodge within you," Jer. 4:14. The mind is the shop where sin is first framed. Sin begins at the thoughts. The thoughts are the first plotters and contrivers of evil. The mind and imagination are the stage where sin is first acted. The malicious man acts over sin in his thoughts, he contemplates revenge. The impure person acts over immorality in his thoughts, he contemplates lust. The Lord humbles us for our contemplative wickedness, Proverbs 30:32. "If you have thought evil, lay your hand upon your mouth." How much sin do men commit in the chamber of their imagination?

Meditating in God's law would be a good means to banish these sinful thoughts. If David had carried the book of the law about him, and meditated in it, he would not have looked on Bathsheba with a lascivious eye, 2 Sam. 2:11. Holy meditation would have quenched that wildfire of lust. The Word of God is pure, Psalm 119:140, not only subjectively—but effectively. It is not only pure in itself—but it makes them pure who meditate in it. Christ whipped the buyers and sellers out of the temple, John 2:15. Holy meditation would whip out idle and vagrant thoughts, and not allow them to lodge in the mind. What is the reason the angels in heaven have not one vain thought? They have a sight of God, their eye is never off him. If the eye of the soul were fixed on God by meditation, how would vain impure thoughts vanish! As when that woman was in the tower, and Abimelech came near to the tower to have entered, but she threw a mill-stone out of the tower upon him, and killed him, Judg, 9:52. Just so, when we have gotten into the high tower of meditation, and sinful thoughts would come near to enter, we may from this tower throw a millstone upon them, and destroy them. And thus you have seen the benefit of meditation.

XVI. The EXCELLENCY of Meditation.

Aristotle places felicity, in the contemplation of the mind. Meditation is highly commended by Augustine, Chrysostom, and Cyprian—as the nursery of piety. Hierom calls it his Paradise. With what words shall I set it forth? Other duties have done excellently—but "you excel them all." Meditation is a friend to all the graces, it helps to water the plantation. I may call it in Basil's expression, the treasury where all the graces are locked up; and with Theophylact, the very gate and portal by which we enter into glory. By meditation the spirits are raised and heightened to a kind of angelic frame. Meditation sweetly puts us in heaven, before we arrive there. Meditation brings God and the soul together, 1 John 3:2.

Meditation is the saints' looking glass, by which they see things invisible. Meditation is the golden ladder by which they ascend to paradise. Meditation is the spy they send abroad to search the land of promise, and it brings a cluster of the grapes of Eshcol with it. Meditation is the dove they send out, and it brings an olive branch of peace in its mouth. But who can tell how sweet honey is, save they that taste it? The excellency of meditation I leave to experienced Christians, who will say the comfort of it may be better felt than expressed.

To excite all to this so useful, excellent (I had almost said angelic) duty, let me lay down some divine motives to meditation; and how glad would I be, if I might revive this duty among Christians.

XVII. Divine MOTIVES to Meditation.

1. Meditation manifests what a man really is. By this he may take a measure of his heart, whether it be good or bad. Proverbs 23:7, "For as he thinks in his heart—so he is." As the meditation is—such is the man. Meditation is the touchstone of a Christian, it shows what metal he is made of. Meditation is a spiritual index. The index shows what is in the book—so meditation shows what is in the heart. If all a man's meditations are how he may get power against sin, how he may grow in grace, how he may have more communion with God; this shows what is in his heart—the frame of his heart is spiritual. By the beating of this pulse, judge of the health of your soul. It is made the character of a godly man—that he fears God, "and thinks on his name," Mal. 3:17. As are the thoughts—such is the heart.

But the thoughts of the ungodly are taken up with pride and lust. "Their thoughts are thoughts of iniquity," Isa, 59:7. When vain sinful thoughts come, ungodly men make much of them, they make room for them, they shall eat and lodge with them. But if a good thought happens to come into their mind, it is soon turned out of doors, as an unwelcome guest; this argues much unsoundness of heart. Let this provoke to holy meditation.

2. The thoughts of God, as they bring delight with them—so they leave peace behind them. Those are the best hours which are spent with God. Conscience, as the bee, gives honey. It will not grieve us when we come to die—that we have spent our time in holy soliloquies and meditations. But what honor will the sinner have, when he shall ask conscience the question as Joram did Jehu, 2 Kings 9:22, "Is it peace, conscience, is it peace?" And conscience shall say as Jehu, "What peace, as long as the whoredoms of your mother Jezebel, and her witchcrafts are so many?" Oh how sad will it be with a man at such a time? Christians, as you desire peace, "meditate in God's law day and night."

This duty of meditation being neglected, the heart will run wild, it will not be a vineyard—but a wilderness.

3. Meditation keeps the heart in a good spiritual health. It plucks up the weeds of sin, it prunes the wasteful branches, it waters the flowers of grace, it sweeps all the walks in the heart, that Christ may walk there with delight. For lack of holy meditation, the heart lies like the sluggard's field, Proverbs 24:31, all overgrown with thorns and briars—with unclean, earthly thoughts. It is rather the devil's hog stye, than Christ's garden. It is like a house fallen to ruin, fit only for unclean spirits to inhabit.

4. The fruitlessness of all worldly meditations. One man lays out his thoughts about laying up money; his meditations are how to raise himself in the world, and when he has arrived at an estate, often God blows upon it, Hag. 1:9. His care is for his child, and perhaps God takes it away, or if it lives, it proves a cross. Another meditates how to satisfy his ambition, "Honor me before the people," 1 Sam. 15:30. Alas, what is honor—but a meteor in the air;

a torch lighted by the breath of people, with the least puff blown out! How many live to see their names buried before them? When this sun is in its meridian splendor—it soon sets in a cloud.

Thus fruitless are those meditations which do not center upon God. It is but to carry dust against the wind. But especially at death; then a man sees all those thoughts which were not spent upon God, to be fruitless, Psalm 146:4. "In that very day his thoughts perish." I may allude to it in this sense—all worldly, vain thoughts, in that day of death perish, and come to nothing! What good will the whole globe of the world do at such a time? Those who have reveled out their thoughts in impertinences, will but be the more disquieted; it will cut them to the heart, to think how they have spun a fool's thread!

A Scythian captain having, for a draught of water, yielded up the city, cried out, "What have I lost!" So will it be with that man when he comes to die, who has spent all his meditations upon the world; he will say, "What have I lost! I have lost heaven, I have betrayed my soul!" And should not the consideration of this fix our minds upon the thoughts of God and glory? All other meditations are fruitless; like a piece of ground which has much cost laid out upon it—but it yields no crop.

5. Holy meditation is never lost. God has a pen to write down all our good thoughts, Mal. 3:5. "A book of remembrance was written for those who thought upon his name." God has all our meditations written in his book. God pens our closet devotion.

6. See the blessedness affixed to the meditating Christian. "Blessed is the man who does not walk in the

counsel of the wicked or stand in the way of sinners or sit in the seat of mockers. But his delight is in the law of the Lord, and on his law he meditates day and night." Psalm 1:1-2. Say not it is hard to meditate. It brings much blessedness. Lycurgus could draw the Lacedemonians to do anything, by giving them rewards. If ungodly men can meditate with delight on that which will make them cursed; shall not we meditate on that which will make us blessed? nay, in the Hebrew it is in the plural, blessednesses, we shall have one blessedness upon another.

7. Delightful meditation in God's law is the best way for a man to prosper in his estate. Josh. 1:8. "This book of the law shall not depart out of your mouth—but you shall meditate therein; for then shall you make your way prosperous." I leave this to their consideration who are desirous to thrive in the world; and let this serve for a motive to meditation.

The next thing remaining, is to lay down some rules about meditation.

XVIII. RULES concerning Meditation.

Rule 1. When you go to meditate—be very SERIOUS in the work. Let there be a deep impression upon your soul. That you may be serious in meditation, do these two things:

1. Get yourself into a posture of holy reverence. Over-awe your heart with the thoughts of God, and the incomprehensibleness of his Majesty. When you are at the work of meditation, remember you are now to deal with GOD. If an angel from heaven did appoint to meet you at such an hour, would you not prepare yourself with all

seriousness and solemnity, to meet him? Behold—a greater than an angel is here; the God of glory is present! He has an eye upon you, he sees the state of your heart when you are alone. Think with yourself, O Christian, when you are going to meditate—that you are now to deal with him in private—before whom the angels adore, and the devils tremble! Think with yourself, that you are now in his presence before whom you must shortly stand and all the world with you—to receive their everlasting sentence. You must die, and how soon you know not; from the closet to the tribunal.

2. That your heart may be serious in meditation, labor to possess your thoughts with the solemnity and greatness of the work you are now going about. As David said concerning his building a house for God—the work is great, 1 Chron. 29:1. So it may be said of meditation—the work is great, and we had need gather and rally together all the powers of the soul to the work! If you were to set about a work wherein your life was concerned, how serious would you be in the thoughts of it? In the business of meditation, your soul is concerned; eternity depends upon it! If you neglect it, or are slight in it—it will have eternal consequences. If Archimedes was so serious in drawing his mathematical line, that he minded not the sacking of the city; O how serious should a Christian be when he is drawing a line for eternity! When you are going to meditate, you are going to the greatest work in the world!

Rule. 2. READ before you meditate. "Do not let this Book of the Law depart from your mouth; meditate on it day and night, so that you may be careful to do everything written in it. Then you will be prosperous and successful." Joshua 1:8. Read before you meditate. The Law must be in Joshua's mouth; he was first to read--and then meditate.

"Give attendance to reading," 1 Timothy 4:13. Then it follows, "meditate on these things," verse 15. Reading furnishes the mind with matter. Reading is the oil which feeds the lamp of meditation. Reading helps to rectify meditation. Augustine well says that, "meditation without reading will be erroneous." Naturally, the mind is defiled, and will be minting thoughts; and how many untruths does it mint! Therefore first read in the book of the Law—and then meditate! Be sure your meditations are grounded upon Scripture.

There is a strange Utopia in the imaginations of some men; they take those for true principles, which are false; and if they mistake their principles they must needs be wrong in their meditations. Thus the mind having laid in wrong principles--the meditation must be erroneous, and a man at last goes to hell upon a mistake! Therefore be sure you read before you meditate--that you may say, "it is written!" Meditate on nothing but what you believe to be a truth; believe nothing to be a truth, but what can show its letters of credence from the Word.

Observe this rule--let reading usher in meditation. Reading without meditation—is unfruitful! Meditation without reading—is dangerous!

Rule 3. Do not multiply the subjects of meditation. That is, meditate not on too many things at once; like the bird that hops from one branch to another, and stays in no one place. Single out rather some one topic at a time, which you will meditate upon. Too much variety distracts. One truth driven home by meditation, will most greatly affect the heart! A man that is to shoot, sets up one target which he aims at to hit. When you are to shoot your mind above the world by meditation, set one thing before you to hit! If you are to meditate on the passion of Christ, let that take up all thoughts! If you are to meditate upon death, confine your thoughts to that. One subject at a time is enough. Martha while she was cumbered about many things, neglected the one needful thing; so while our meditations are taken up about many things, we lose that one thing which should affect our hearts, and do us more good. Drive but one wedge of meditation at a time—but be sure you drive it home to the heart. Those who aim at a whole flock of birds hit none. Several medicines taken together, the one hinders the virtue of the other; whereas a single medicine might do good.

Rule 4. To meditation, join EXAMINATION. When you have been meditating on any spiritual subject, put an enquiry to your soul, and though it is short, let it be serious. "O my soul, is it thus with you—or not?" When you have been meditating about the fear of God—that it is the "beginning of wisdom"—make an enquiry, "O my soul, is this fear planted in your heart? You are almost come to the end of your days, are you yet come to the beginning of wisdom?" When you have been meditating on Christ, his virtues, his privileges, make an enquiry, "O my soul, do you love him who is so lovely; and are you ingrafted into him? Are you a living branch of this living vine?" When you have been meditating upon the graces of the Spirit, make an enquiry, "O my soul, are you adorned as the bride of Christ with this chain of pearl? Have you your certificate for heaven ready? Will my graces be to seek, when I should have them to show?" Thus should a Christian in his retirements, parley often with his heart.

For lack of this examination, meditation evaporates and comes to nothing. For lack of examination while in meditation, many are strangers to their own hearts; though they live known to others, they die unknown to themselves. Meditation is like a telescope by which we contemplate heavenly objects; but self-examination is like a looking glass by which we see into our own souls, and can judge how it is with us. Meditation joined with examination, is like the sun on the dial, which shows how the day goes, it shows us how our hearts stand affected to spiritual things.

Rule 5. Seal up meditation with PRAYER. Pray over your meditations. Prayer sanctifies everything; without prayer they are but unhallowed meditations. Prayer fastens meditation upon the soul. Prayer is a tying a knot at the end of meditation—so that it does not slip. Pray that God will keep those holy meditations in your mind forever, that the savor of them may abide upon your hearts, 1 Chron. 29:18. "O Lord, keep this desire in the hearts of your people forever, and keep their hearts loyal to you." So let us pray, that when we have been musing on heavenly things, and our hearts have waxed hot within us, we may not cool into a sinful tepidness and lukewarmness—but that our affections may be as the lamp of the sanctuary—always burning.

Rule 6. The last rule is, let meditation be reduced to PRACTICE. Live out your meditation. "Do not let this Book of the Law depart from your mouth; meditate on it day and night, so that you may be careful to do everything written in it. Then you will be prosperous and successful." Joshua 1:8. Meditation and practice, like two sisters, must go hand in hand. Cassian says, that "the contemplative life cannot be perfected without the practice." We read that the angels had wings, and hands under their wings, Ezek. 1:8. It may be an emblem of this truth; Christians must not only fly upon the wing of meditation—but they must be active in obedience, they must have hands under their wings! The end of meditation is action. We must not only meditate in God's law—but walk in his law, Deut. 28:9. Without this, we are like those Gnostics, who had much knowledge—but were licentious in their lives. Christians must be like the sun, which does not only send forth heat—but goes its circuit round the world. It is not enough that the affections are heated by meditation—but we must go our circuit too, that is, move regularly in the sphere of obedience. After warming at the fire of meditation, we must be fitter for work. Meditation is the life of piety; and practice is the life of meditation. It is said in the honor of Gregory Nazianzen, that he lived out his own sermons. So a godly Christian must live out his own meditations. For instance:

1. When you have been meditating on sin, which, for its bitterness, is compared to grapes of gall; for its damnableness to poison of asps, and you begin to burn in a holy indignation against sin—now put your meditations in practice—give sin a bill of divorce, Job 11:14. "If iniquity is in your hand, put it far away, and let not wickedness dwell in your tabernacles."

2. When you have been meditating on the graces of the Spirit, let the verdure and luster of these graces be seen in you. Live these graces. Meditate, "that you may observe and do." It was Paul's counsel to Timothy, "Exercise yourself to godliness." Meditation and practice are like a pair of compasses, the one part of the compass fixes upon the center, and the other part goes round the circumference. Just so, a Christian by meditation fixes upon God as the center, and by practice goes around the circumference of the commandments.

A man who has let his thoughts run out upon riches, will not only have them in the notion—but will endeavor to get riches. Let your meditation be practical. When you have been meditating upon a promise, live upon a promise. When you have been meditating on a good conscience, never leave until you can say as Paul, "Herein I exercise myself, to have a good conscience," Acts 24:16. Beloved, here lies the very essence of true religion.

That this rule may be well observed, consider,

1. It is only the practical part of religion, which will make a man blessed. Meditation is a beautiful flower—but Rachel said to her husband: "Give me children or I die," Gen. 30:1. So, If meditation is barren, and does not bring forth the child of obedience—it will die and come to nothing!

2. If when you have meditated in God's law, you do not obey his law, you will come short of those who have come short of heaven. It is said of Herod, Mark 6:20, "He did many things;" he was in many things a practicer of John's ministry. Those who meditate in God's law, and do not practice it, are not so good as Herod. Nay, they are no better than the devil; he knows much—but still he is a devil.

3. Meditation without practice will increase a man's condemnation. If a father writes a letter to his son, and the son shall read over this letter, and study it—yet not do as his father writes, this would be an aggravation of his fault, and would but provoke his father the more against him. Thus when we have meditated upon the evil of sin, and the beauty of holiness—yet we do not eschew the one, nor espouse the other, it will but incense the divine Majesty so much the more against us, and we shall "be beaten with many stripes."

Printed in Great Britain
by Amazon

27168944R00046